Y0-AGL-585

Water Planet

Developed at
Lawrence Hall of Science
University of California at Berkeley

Published and Distributed by **Delta Education**,
a member of the School Specialty Family

© 2009 by The Regents of the University of California. All rights reserved. No part of this book may be reproduced or transmitted in any form or by any means, electronic or mechanical, including photocopying or recording, or by any information storage and retrieval system, without permission in writing from the publisher.

1012452
978-1-59821-789-6
1 2 3 4 5 6 QUE 13 12 11 10 09 08

The FOSS program began at the Lawrence Hall of Science as a science enrichment program. Over the past 25 years, with the support of the National Science Foundation and the University of California at Berkeley, the program has evolved into a total curriculum for all students and their teachers, grades K–6. The program reflects significant contributions of dedicated professionals in the classroom, their students, administrators, parents, and members of the scientific community. We acknowledge the thousands of educators who have given life to the ideas embodied in the FOSS program. We acknowledge and thank them all for their contributions to the development and implementation of FOSS.

FOSS © 2009 and © 2007 Lawrence Hall of Science Team

Larry Malone and Linda De Lucchi, FOSS Project Codirectors and Lead Developers; Kathy Long, Assessment Coordinator; Teri Dannenberg, Developer; Susan Kaschner Jagoda, Developer; Ann Moriarty, Developer; Kimi Hosoume, Developer; Deanne Giffin, Early Childhood Consultant; Joanna Totino, EL Consultant and Professional Developer; Jaine Kopp and Jenny Maguire, Mathematics Consultants; David Lippman, Editor and Program Specialist; Carol Sevilla, Publications Design Coordinator; Rose Craig, Illustrator; Susan Stanley and Carol Bevilacqua, Graphic Production; Susan Ketchner, Multimedia Director; Alana Chan, Nicole Alexis Medina, and Kate Jordan, FOSSweb Producers; Roseanna Yau and Leigh Anne McConnaughey, Multimedia Artist and Designer; Dan Bluestein, Programmer; Roger Vang, Programmer; Christopher Cianciarulo, Programmer; John Quick, Photographer

FOSS © 2009 and © 2007 Delta Education Team

Bonnie Piotrowski, FOSS Editorial Director
Project Team: Jennifer Apt, Mathew Bacon, Lynne Bleeker, Tom Guetling, Joann Hoy, Lisa Lachance, Elizabeth Luzadre, Paulette Miley, Sandra Mitchell, Cathrine Monson, Cyndy Patrick, John Prescott, Gary Standafer, Heidi Tyson, Nina Whitney

FOSS © 2009 and © 2007 Content Reviewers

David M. Andrews, EdD, Professor of Biology and Science Education and Executive Director, Science and Mathematics Education Center, California State University, Fresno, CA
Carol Balfe, PhD, Science Education Consultant and Former Research Scientist, Oakland, CA
Ellen P. Metzger, PhD, Professor of Geology, California State University, San Jose, CA

FOSS © 2009 and © 2007 Teacher Reviewers

Amy Edmindson, Centralia School, Anaheim, CA; Amy Hellewell, Bonita Canyon School, Irvine, CA; Bonney Waters, Two Bunch Palms Elementary, Desert Hot Springs, CA; Christina Lambie, Highland Elementary, Richmond, CA; Debby Palmer, Turtle Rock Elementary, Irvine, CA; Heinrich Sartin, District 2 Office, North Hollywood, CA; Jeff Self, Washington Elementary, Eureka, CA; Jennifer Faulhaber, G. H. Dysinger School, Buena Park, CA; Jill Garmon, Brywood Elementary, Irvine, CA; Don McKenney, Oakland Unified School District, Oakland, CA; Jill Miles, Sheridan School, Sheridan, CA; Jim Jones, Valley View School, Coachella, CA; Joy Peoples, Riverside School, Riverside, CA; Katherine Jacobs, Verde School, Irvine, CA; Kathy Albrecht, Heritage Oak School, Roseville, CA; Lauren Vu-Tran, Fountain Valley School, Fountain Valley, CA; Lillian Valadez-Rodela, San Pedro MST, San Pedro, CA; Lori Van-Gorp, Anaheim Hills Elementary, Anaheim, CA; Maura Crossin, Local District 4, Los Angeles, CA; Melissa Tallman, College Park Elementary, Irvine, CA; Nancy Lester, Newport Elementary, Newport Beach, CA; Pamela Rockwell, Anaheim Hills Elementary, Anaheim, CA; Rhonda Lemon, Danbrook School, Anaheim, CA; Sherri Ferguson, Brywood Elementary, Irvine, CA; Susan Liberati, Beverly Hills School District, Beverly Hills, CA; Will Neddersen, Tustin USD, Tustin, CA

Production for © 2007 and © 2003 Editions

LaurelTech Integrated Publishing Services

FOSS © 1993–2003 Edition Staff and Contributors

Professor Lawrence F. Lowery, Principal Investigator; Linda De Lucchi, Codirector; Larry Malone, Codirector; Kathy Long, Assessment Coordinator; Leigh Agler, Developer; Susan Kaschner Jagoda, Developer; Kari Rees, Reading Consultant; Carol Sevilla, Graphic Designer; Rose Craig, Illustrator
Contributors: Sara Armstrong, John Quick, Eileen Massey, Joanna Totino, Denise Soderlund, Laura Loutit, Eric Crane, Yiyu Xie, Marco Molinaro, Susan Ketchner, Joannan Gladden, Lisa Haderlie-Baker, Sandra Ragan, Cheryl Webb, Alev Burton, Mark Warren, Marshall Montgomery

FOSS © 2000–2003 Delta Education Team

Mathew Bacon, Grant Gardner, Tom Guetling, Joann Hoy, Dana Koch, Lisa Lachance, Cathrine Monson, Kerri O'Donnell, Bonnie Piotrowski, John Prescott, Jeanette Wall

FOSS Grades K–6 Revision © 2000-2003 Teacher Associates
Claire Kelley, Dennett Elementary School, Plympton, MA
Dyan Van Bishler, Clyde Hill Elementary, Bellevue, WA
Sig Doran, Clyde Hill Elementary, Bellevue, WA
Ann Kumata, John Muir Elementary, Seattle, WA
Kate Shonk, Pleasant Valley Primary, Vancouver, WA
Theresa Fowler, John Rogers Elementary, Seattle, WA
Andrea Edwards, Woodland Primary School, Woodland, WA
Deanne Giffin and Janet Gay, Bancroft Elementary School, Walnut Creek, CA
Jill Kraus, Hawthorne Elementary School, Oakland, CA
Brenda Redmond, Los Perales School, Moraga, CA
Catherine Behymer, Napa Valley Language Academy, Napa, CA
Alison McSweeney, Dennett Elementary, Plympton, MA
Helen Howard and Carol Strandberg, Mt. Erie Elementary, Anacortes, WA
Rondi Peth, Dawn Mayer, and Jeannette Beatty, Fidalgo Elementary, Anacortes, WA
Virginia Kammer, Fresno Unified School District, Fresno, CA
Henrietta Griffitts and Jackie Meylan Dodge, Mt. Diablo Unified School District

Production for © 2000 Edition *FOSS Science Stories*
Creative Media Applications, Inc.
Rhea Baehr, Writer; Michael Burgan, Writer; Robin Doak, Writer; Matthew Dylan, Writer; Emily Lauren, Writer; Matt Levine, Editor; Joanne Mattern, Writer; Dona Smith, Writer; Fabia Wargin, Graphic Design

Original FOSS © 1993–1995 Grades K–6 School District Partners
Kathy Jacobsen, Mt. Diablo Unified School District
Judy Guilkey-Amado and Alexa Hauser, Vallejo City Unified School District
Richard Merrill, Mt. Diablo Unified School District

**Original FOSS © 1993–1995 Grades K–6 National Trials Center Directors and Advisers
Directors:**
Ramona Anshutz, Kansas State Dept. of Education; Ron Bonnstetter, University of
Nebraska; John Cairns, Delaware Dept. of Public Instruction; Arthur Camins, CSD #16,
Brooklyn, NY; Winston Hoskins, Garland Independent School District, TX; Rhoda Immer,
Siskiyou, County Office of Education, CA; Mildred Jones, New York City Schools;
Floyd Mattheis, East Carolina University, NC; Alan McCormack, San Diego State
University; Don McCurdy, University of Nebraska; Joseph Premo, Minneapolis Schools;
John Staver, Kansas State University, Manhattan, KS; Brian Swagerty, Siskiyou County
Office of Education, CA; Sandra Wolford, Colonial School District, New Castle, DE

Advisers:
Sara Armstrong, Heidi Bachman, Carl Berger, Donna Dailey, Robert Dean, Steve Essig, Rosella
Jackson, Marsha Knudsen, Catherine Koshland, Samuel Markowitz, Glenn McGlathery, Margaret
McIntyre, Shirley McKinney, Richard Merrill, Marshall Montgomery, Gary Nakagiri, Karen Ostlund,
John Schippers, Dave Stronck, Dean Taylor, Judy Van Hoorn

FOSS © 1993–1995 Grades K–6 National Trials Leadership Partners
David Allard, Hal Benham, Diane Benham, Arthur Camins, Vicki Clark, John Clementson, Cathy
Klinesteker, Karen Dawkins, Sally Dudley, Sheila Dunston, Steve Essig, Fred Fifer, Theresa
Flaningam, Chris Foster, Robert Grossman, Cynthia Ledbetter, Charlotte McDonald, Karen Ostlund,
Janet Posen, Carlton Robardey, Twyla Sherman, Gerald Skoog, Dean Taylor, Mary Zapata

Published and Distributed by Delta Education, a member of the School Specialty Family

The FOSS program was developed in part with the support of the National Science Foundation grant
nos. MDR-8751727 and MDR-9150097. However, any opinions, findings, conclusions, statements, and
recommendations expressed herein are those of the authors and do not necessarily reflect the views of NSF.

Copyright © 2009 by The Regents of the University of California
All rights reserved. Any part of this work (other than duplication masters) may not be reproduced
or transmitted in any form or by any means, electronic or mechanical, including photocopying and
recording, or by an information storage or retrieval system without permission of the University of
California. For permission please write to: FOSS Project, Lawrence Hall of Science, University of
California, Berkeley, CA 94720.

Table of Contents

A Tour of the Solar System

Make believe you are coming to the **solar system** as a stranger. You are on a tour. There is a tour guide to provide information. You have a window to look out. The tour is about to start. What will you see?

The first view of the solar system is from space. From here the whole solar system can be seen. The most surprising thing is that the solar system is mostly empty. The matter is concentrated in tiny dots. And the dots are far apart. Most of the dots are **planets.** From far away, that is what you see.

There is a **star** in the center of the solar system. Four small planets **orbit** pretty close to the star. These are the rocky **terrestrial planets.**

Next there is a region of small bits of matter orbiting the star. This is the **asteroid** belt.

Out farther, four big gas planets orbit the star. These are the **gas giants.**

Beyond the gas giants is a huge region of different-size icy chunks of matter called the **Kuiper Belt.** Some of the chunks are big enough to be planets. Others have orbits that send them flying through the rest of the solar system. That's all that can be seen from out in space.

Sizes and distances of solar-system objects are not drawn to scale.

The Sun

The **Sun** is a star. It is just like the stars you can see in the night sky. The Sun is at the center of the solar system. Everything else in the solar system orbits the Sun. The Sun rules.

Earth

The Sun is an average star. It is much like millions of other stars in the **Milky Way** galaxy. The Sun formed about 5 billion years ago. A cloud of gas began to spin. As it spun, it formed a sphere. The sphere got smaller and smaller. As it got smaller, it got hotter. Eventually the sphere got so hot it started to radiate light and heat. A star was born.

The Sun is made mostly of **hydrogen** (72%) and **helium** (26%). And it is huge. The diameter is about 1,384,000 kilometers (860,000 miles). The **diameter** is the distance from one side of the Sun to the other through the center. That's about 109 times the diameter of Earth. (See Earth compared to the Sun at the bottom of the picture on the left.)

The Sun is incredibly hot. Scientists have figured out that the temperature at the center of the Sun is 15,000,000°C (27,000,000°F). The temperature of the Sun's surface is lower, about 5,500°C (10,000°F). Hydrogen atoms constantly combine to form helium atoms in **thermonuclear reactions.** These reactions create heat and light energy. About 3.6 tons of the Sun's **mass** is being changed into heat and light every second. This energy radiates out from the Sun in all directions. A small amount of it falls on Earth.

Another name for the Sun is Sol. That's why the whole system of planets is called the solar system. The solar system is named for the ruling star. The reason the Sun rules is its size. The Sun has 99.8% of the total mass of the solar system. All the other solar-system objects travel around the Sun in **predictable** almost-circular paths called orbits. The most obvious objects orbiting the Sun are the planets.

Terrestrial Planets

The terrestrial planets are the four planets closest to the Sun. The terrestrial planets are small and rocky.

Relative sizes of the terrestrial planets

Mercury

Mercury is closest to the Sun. Mercury is smaller than Earth and has no **satellite** (moon). By human standards, it is an uninviting place. Mercury is very hot on the side facing the Sun and very cold on the dark side. It has no atmosphere or water.

Mercury is covered with craters. The **craters** are the result of thousands of collisions with objects flying through space. The surface of Mercury looks a lot like Earth's Moon.

Planet Mercury is closest to the Sun.

Venus

Venus is the second planet from the Sun. Venus is about the same size as Earth and has no satellites. The surface of Venus is very hot all the time. It is hot enough to melt lead, making it one of the hottest places in the solar system.

There is no liquid water on Venus. But Venus does have an atmosphere of carbon dioxide. The dense, cloudy atmosphere makes it impossible to see the planet's surface. Modern radar, however, allows scientists to take pictures through the clouds. We now know that the surface of Venus is dry, cracked, and covered with volcanoes.

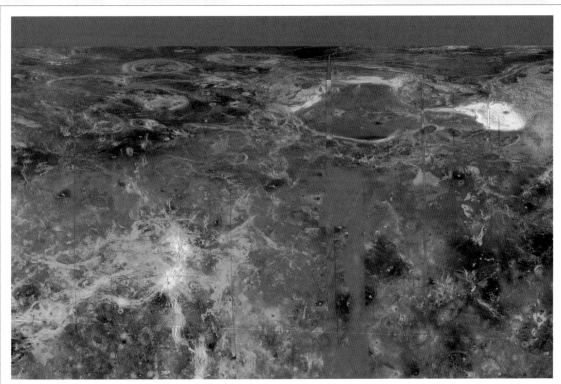

The surface of Venus is hot and cratered.

Earth is the third planet from the Sun. Earth has a moderate (mild) temperature all the time. It has an atmosphere of nitrogen and oxygen, and it has liquid water. As far as we know, Earth is the only place in the universe that has life. Earth also has one large satellite called the **Moon,** or Luna. The Moon orbits Earth once a month. The Moon is responsible for the tides in Earth's oceans. The Moon is the only **extraterrestrial** place humans have visited.

Moon

Earth is 150 million kilometers (93 million miles) from the Sun. This is a huge distance. It's hard to imagine that distance, but think about this. Sit in one end zone of a football field and curl up into a ball. You are the Sun. A friend goes to the other end zone and holds up the eraser from a pencil. That's Earth. Get the idea? Earth is tiny, and it is a long distance from the Sun. Still, the solar energy that reaches Earth provides the right amount of energy for life as we know it.

Mars

Mars is the fourth planet from the Sun and has two small satellites, Phobos and Deimos. Mars is a little like Earth, except it is smaller, colder, and drier. There are some places on Mars that are like Death Valley in California. Other places on Mars are more like Antarctica and the volcanoes of Hawaii.

Mars is sometimes called the Red Planet because of its red soil. The soil contains iron oxide, or rust. The iron oxide in the soil tells scientists that Mars probably had liquid water at one time. But liquid water has not been on Mars for 3.5 billion years. It has frozen water in polar ice caps that grow and shrink with the seasons on Mars.

Mars is the next likely place humans will visit. But exploring Mars will not be easy. Humans can't breathe the thin atmosphere of carbon dioxide. And explorers will need to wear life-support spacesuits for protection against the cold.

Several robotic landers, such as *Viking, Spirit, Opportunity,* and *Sojourner,* have observed Mars and sent back information about the surface and possibility of water. There is evidence that there is a lot of frozen water just under the surface.

Water frost on the surface of Mars

Asteroids

Beyond the orbit of Mars there are millions of chunks of rock and iron called asteroids. They all orbit the Sun in a region called the asteroid belt. The asteroid belt is like the boundary of the terrestrial planets. The planets farther out are quite different from the terrestrial planets.

Asteroid Ida with satellite Dactyl

Some asteroids even have moons. When the spacecraft *Galileo* flew past asteroid Ida in 1993, scientists were surprised to find it had a satellite. They named the tiny moon Dactyl. The largest object in the asteroid belt is Ceres, a **dwarf planet.** It is about 960 kilometers (600 miles) around.

Gas Giants

The next four planets are the gas giants. They do not have rocky surfaces like the terrestrial planets. So there is no place to land or walk around on them. They are much bigger than the terrestrial planets. What we have learned about the gas giants has come from probes sent out to fly by and orbit around them. Even though the gas giants are all made of gas, each one is different.

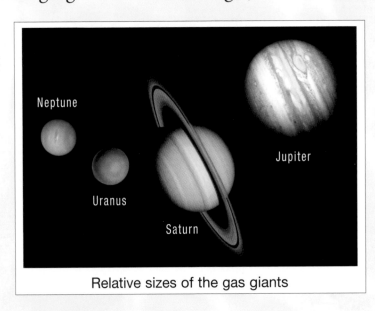
Relative sizes of the gas giants

Jupiter

Jupiter is the fifth planet from the Sun. Jupiter is the largest planet in the solar system. It is 11 times larger in diameter than Earth. Sixty-three moons have been found to orbit Jupiter. The four largest moons are Ganymede, Callisto, Io, and Europa.

Jupiter's atmosphere is cold and poisonous. It is mostly hydrogen and helium. The stripes and swirls on Jupiter's surface are cold, windy clouds of ammonia and water. Its Great Red Spot is a giant storm as wide as three Earths. This storm has been raging for hundreds of years. On Jupiter, the atmospheric pressure is so strong it squishes gas into liquid. Jupiter's atmosphere could crush a metal spaceship like a paper cup.

Ganymede

Europa

Jupiter

Io

Callisto

9

Saturn

Saturn

Saturn is the sixth planet from the Sun. Saturn is the second biggest planet and is very cold. There are at least 60 satellites orbiting Saturn. Saturn is made up mostly of hydrogen, helium, and methane. It doesn't have a solid surface. It has clouds and storms like Jupiter, but they are harder to see because they move so fast. Winds in Saturn's upper atmosphere reach 1,825 kilometers per hour (1,135 miles per hour).

The most dramatic feature of Saturn is its ring system. The largest ring reaches out 200,000 kilometers (125,000 miles) from Saturn's surface. The rings are made of billions of small chunks of ice and rock. All the gas giants have rings, but the others are not as spectacular as Saturn's.

Close-up of the rings of Saturn

Uranus

Uranus is the seventh planet from the Sun. Uranus has 27 moons and 11 rings. Uranus is very cold and windy, and would be poisonous to humans. It is smaller and colder than Saturn.

Uranus has clouds that are extremely cold at the top. Below the cloud tops there is a layer of extremely hot water, ammonia, and methane. Near its core, Uranus heats up to 4,982°C (9,000°F). Uranus appears blue because of the methane gas in its atmosphere.

Neptune

Uranus

Neptune

Neptune is the eighth planet from the Sun. Neptune has 13 moons and 4 thin rings. Neptune is the smallest of the gas giants, but is still the fourth largest planet in the solar system.

Neptune is made mostly of hydrogen and helium with some methane. Neptune may be the windiest planet in the solar system. Winds rip through the clouds at more than 2,000 kilometers per hour (1,200 miles per hour). Scientists think there might be an ocean of super-hot water under Neptune's cold clouds. It does not boil away, because of the incredible pressure.

Kuiper Belt

Pluto

Out beyond the gas giants is a disk-shaped zone of icy objects called the Kuiper Belt. Some of the objects are fairly large. **Pluto** is one of the Kuiper Belt objects. Some scientists considered Pluto a planet because it is massive enough to pull itself into a sphere. Others did not consider Pluto a planet. To them, Pluto was just one of the large pieces of debris in the Kuiper Belt. Scientists now call Pluto a dwarf planet.

Pluto has a thin atmosphere. It is so cold on Pluto that the atmosphere actually freezes and falls to Pluto's surface when it is farthest from the Sun. Even though Pluto is smaller than Earth's Moon, it has its own satellite. It is called Charon and is about half the size of Pluto.

Pluto and its moon Charon

Eris

In July 2005, astronomers at the California Institute of Technology announced the discovery of a new planet-like object. It is called Eris. Like Pluto, Eris is a Kuiper Belt object and a dwarf planet. But Eris is more than twice as far away from the Sun as Pluto! The picture to the right is an artist's idea of what the Sun would look like from a position close to Eris.

A painting showing that the Sun would look like a bright star from Eris

Comets

Comets are big chunks of ice, rock, and gas. Sometimes comets are compared to dirty snowballs. Scientists think comets might have valuable information about the origins of the solar system.

Comets orbit the Sun in long, oval paths. Most of them travel way beyond the orbit of Pluto. A comet's trip around the Sun can take hundreds or even millions of years, depending on its orbit. A comet's tail shows up as it nears the Sun and begins to warm. The gases and dust that form the comet's tail always point away from the Sun.

Comets have been called dirty snowballs.

Comet orbits can cross those of the planets. In July 1994 a large comet, named Comet Shoemaker-Levy 9, was on a collision course with Jupiter. As it got close to Jupiter, the comet broke into 21 pieces.

Comet Shoemaker-Levy 9 broke into pieces as it got close to Jupiter.

The pieces slammed into Jupiter for a week. Each impact created a crater in Jupiter's surface larger than planet Earth.

Two of the 21 larger than Earth-size craters on Jupiter

Review Questions

1. What is the Sun and what is it made of?

2. What is the solar system?

3. Which planets are terrestrial planets? Which planets are gas giants?

4. What is the Kuiper Belt and what is found there?

5. Which planet has the most moons orbiting it?

6. How are asteroids and comets alike and different?

Ramon E. Lopez

As strange as it may sound, there is weather in space. But it's not weather like we have on Earth. There are no clouds, hurricanes, or snowstorms in space. Space weather is the result of activities on the Sun. The Sun is always radiating energy into the solar system. The regular flow of light and gases is called **solar wind.** But what happens when the Sun goes through a period of violent solar flares? That's what Dr. Ramon E. Lopez (1959–) studies.

Ramon E. Lopez

Solar flares, which are huge solar explosions, send intense blasts of electrified gas into Earth's atmosphere. The blasts can produce electric effects in the atmosphere and on Earth's surface. The electricity can disable satellites orbiting Earth and interfere with radio transmissions and cell-phone operation. Space weather can cause blackouts over large areas.

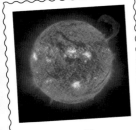

Sun with a large flare

Lopez and his team understand how space weather can damage communication and navigation systems. And they understand how important these systems are to modern society. Will Lopez be able to predict the space weather? Will he be able to warn the world when a dangerous storm is coming from the Sun? Lopez believes that the team he works with may be able to develop a computer program to predict space weather about 30 minutes before it hits Earth. And that may be just long enough to take steps to protect communication and navigation systems from damage.

Why Doesn't Earth Fly Off into Space?

Earth travels around the Sun in a predictable, almost-circular path once a year. That's a distance of about 942 million kilometers (584 million miles) each year. That's an incredible 2.6 million kilometers (1.6 million miles) each day! That's fast.

One important thing to know about objects in motion is that they travel only in straight lines. Objects don't change direction or follow curved paths unless a force pushes or pulls them in a new direction. If nothing pushed or pulled on Earth, it would fly off into space in a straight line.

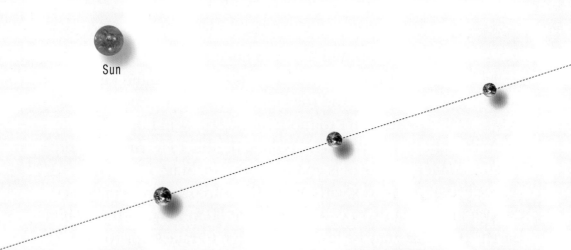

Sun

But Earth doesn't fly straight off into space. Earth travels in a circular path around the Sun. In order to travel a circular path, Earth has to change direction all the time. Something has to push or pull Earth to change its direction. What is pushing or pulling our planet Earth? **Gravity.**

Gravity is the force of attraction between masses. The Sun is a mass. Earth is a mass. The force of attraction between the Sun and Earth pulls hard enough to change Earth's direction of travel.

Remember the string-and-ball demonstration? The hand pulled on the string. The string pulled on the ball. The ball traveled in a circular orbit. Gravity is like the string. The **gravitational attraction** between the Sun and Earth pulls on Earth, changing its direction of travel. That's why Earth travels in a circular orbit around the Sun.

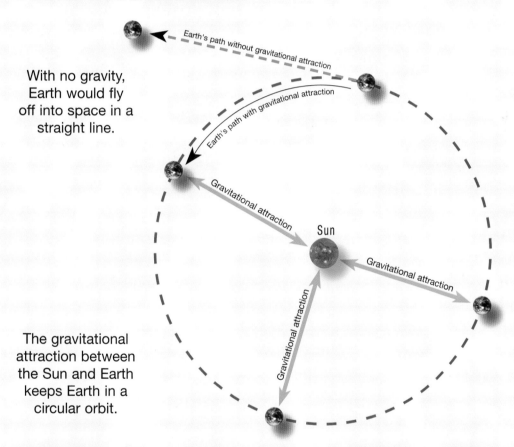

Earth's path without gravitational attraction

With no gravity, Earth would fly off into space in a straight line.

Earth's path with gravitational attraction

Gravitational attraction

Sun

Gravitational attraction

Gravitational attraction

The gravitational attraction between the Sun and Earth keeps Earth in a circular orbit.

Sun's gravity keeps all the planets in their orbits. Otherwise, the planets would fly in straight lines right out of the solar system.

Review Questions

1. **Why do planets stay in orbit around the Sun?**

2. **How is a ball on a string like a planet in its orbit?**

3. **What keeps the Moon in its orbit around Earth?**

Mae Jemison: Astronaut

Mae Jemison, astronaut

Dr. Mae Jemison (1956–) was born in Decatur, Alabama. She moved to Chicago, Illinois, as a child, where an uncle introduced her to **astronomy.** In high school Jemison began reading books on astronomy and space travel. She was only 16 years old when she entered college. She earned degrees in chemical engineering and African and Afro-American studies from Stanford University. She went on to earn her medical degree from Cornell University.

After becoming a doctor, Jemison spent time in western Africa as a Peace Corps physician. But she continued to think about astronomy and space travel. She wanted to be part of the space program.

The official patch of shuttle mission STS-47

Jemison was admitted into the astronaut program in 1987. On September 12, 1992, Jemison became the first African-American woman in space. She was a science mission specialist on the space shuttle *Endeavour.* Jemison conducted experiments to find out more about the effects of being in space. She studied motion sickness, calcium loss in bones, and weightlessness.

Space shuttle mission STS-47 was the 50th space shuttle flight, but only the second flight for the *Endeavour*. The shuttle was in space for 8 days. During those 8 days, Jemison orbited Earth 127 times at an altitude of 307 kilometers (191 miles). The shuttle traveled 5,234,950 kilometers (3,245,669 miles).

Does the space shuttle actually fly in space? Not really. It orbits Earth in the upper atmosphere. In the picture to the right, you can see how close the shuttle is to Earth's surface when it is in orbit. What keeps the shuttle in orbit?

The space shuttle in orbit

Again, gravity. The shuttle travels very fast. Earth's gravity pulls on the shuttle, constantly changing the shuttle's direction of travel. Engineers from the National Aeronautics and Space Administration (NASA) have figured out exactly how fast the shuttle must travel and how high it must be above Earth's surface. They know how strong the force of gravity is. With these data, the space shuttle stays in orbit until the astronauts change the shuttle's speed. Then gravity pulls the shuttle back to Earth. Mission complete.

Space shuttle orbit

Summary: Solar System

The **Milky Way** galaxy has hundreds of billions of **stars.** We live just 150 million kilometers (93 million miles) from one of them. That star is Sol, our **Sun.**

The Sun is not alone. **Planets, dwarf planets, satellites, asteroids, comets,** and other objects travel in **orbits** around the Sun. The Sun and all the bodies that circle it make up the **solar system.**

The Sun

The Sun is by far the largest object in the solar system. It accounts for 99.8% of the mass in the whole solar system. And the Sun is about 109 times bigger than **Earth** in diameter. But unlike Earth, the Sun is made mostly of **hydrogen** (72%) and **helium** (26%). The light and heat radiating from the Sun are created as hydrogen atoms combine to make helium.

The Sun is an average star.

The Planets

Planets are large natural objects that orbit the Sun. There are two major groups of planets in the solar system. Mercury, Venus, Earth, and Mars are **terrestrial planets.** They are close to the Sun, small, and made of rock. Mercury and Venus have no satellites. Earth has one moon, and Mars has two.

Jupiter, Saturn, Uranus, and Neptune are **gas giants.** The gas giants are far from the Sun, huge, and made of gas. Nothing can land on the surface of a gas giant. They all have rings surrounding them, but Saturn's rings are the easiest to see. All the gas giants have moons. Jupiter, the largest of the solar-system planets, has the most moons, 63. Neptune has the fewest, 13.

Pluto is a small, icy body beyond the orbits of the gas giants. It is in a region of icy debris called the **Kuiper Belt.** Pluto is smaller than Earth's **Moon.**

Other Solar-System Objects

The small terrestrial planets are separated from the gas giants by the asteroid belt. This is a collection of millions of rocky chunks orbiting the Sun. Occasionally one gets knocked out of orbit. Some of the most interesting solar-system objects are comets. They come from the Kuiper Belt or even farther out. Comets have large oval orbits that only rarely bring them into the inner solar system. Some comets come back close to the Sun after a million years.

Everything Goes Around

Moving objects travel in straight lines unless a force acts to change their direction. Planets are moving objects. They should travel in straight lines and fly out of the solar system. But the planets don't fly off into space because Sun's **gravity** pulls on the planets and changes their direction of travel. The result is almost-circular orbits around the Sun.

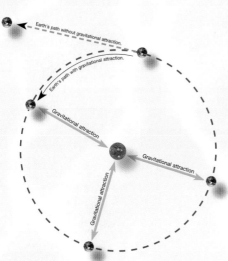

21

Planets of the Solar System

Mercury

Venus

Earth

Mars

Relative sizes of planets

Jupiter

Saturn

Uranus

Pluto
(dwarf planet)

Neptune

Summary Questions

Now is a good time to review what you have recorded in your science notebook. Think about the solar system and the objects that are found in it.

1. **What are the main objects in the solar system? How are they alike or different?**

2. **What is the Sun? What is it made of? What is its role in the solar system?**

3. **Why do the planets and other objects in the solar system stay in their orbits?**

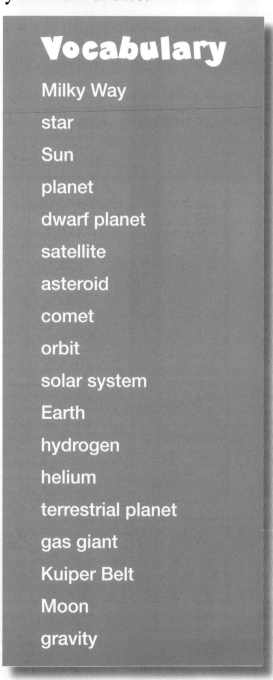

Vocabulary

Milky Way

star

Sun

planet

dwarf planet

satellite

asteroid

comet

orbit

solar system

Earth

hydrogen

helium

terrestrial planet

gas giant

Kuiper Belt

Moon

gravity

Extensions

Math Problem of the Week

Jaine, who is 10, is curious about how old she would be on other planets in the solar system. She knows that on Earth a year equals 365 days. But other planets have longer or shorter years. How can she figure out how old she would be on these planets?

1. How many Earth days old is Jaine?

2. How many Mercury years old is Jaine?

3. How many Mars years old is Jaine?

4. On which planets is Jaine less than a year old?

5. On which planets is Jaine older than she is on Earth?

PLANET	ORBIT IN EARTH DAYS
Mercury	88
Venus	225
Mars	687
Jupiter	4,333
Saturn	10,759
Uranus	30,685
Neptune	60,189
Pluto (dwarf planet)	90,465

Home/School Connection

What solar-system objects can you see in the night sky? Only one star is a solar-system object, our Sun. But it can't be seen in the night sky.

Four solar-system objects can be seen easily with your bare eyes at night. They are the Moon, Venus, Mars, and Jupiter. They are brighter than the stars. But you have to know when and where to look for them. They aren't visible all night, every night.

Two more planets can be seen with bare eyes if you know where to look, Mercury and Saturn. They are only as bright as stars.

Look for solar-system time and place information in the newspaper or on the Internet. Stardate is a good site. Go to www.stardate.org and then go to stargazing/planet viewing. See how many solar-system objects you can find in the night sky.

Drying Up

You know when something is wet. It is covered with water, or it has soaked up a lot of water. When it rains, everything outside gets wet. When you go swimming, you and your swimsuit get wet. Clothes are wet when they come out of the washer, and a dog is wet after a bath.

But things don't stay wet forever. Things get dry, often by themselves. An hour or two after the rain stops, porches, sidewalks, and plants are dry. After a break from swimming to eat lunch, you and your swimsuit are dry. After a few hours on the clothesline, clothes are dry. A dog is dry and fluffy after a short time. Where does the water go?

The water **evaporates.** When water evaporates, it changes from water in its **liquid** form to water in its **gas** form. The gas form of water is called **water vapor.** The water vapor leaves the wet object and goes into the **air.** As the water evaporates, the wet object gets dry.

What happens when you put a wet object in a sealed container? It stays wet. If you put your wet swimsuit in a plastic bag, it's still wet when you take it out of the bag. Why? A little bit of the water in your suit evaporates, but it can't escape into the air. The water vapor has no place to go, so your suit is still wet when you get home.

Have you ever seen water vapor in the air? No, water vapor is invisible. When water changes into vapor, it changes into individual **water molecules.** Water molecules are too small to be seen. The water molecules move into the air among the nitrogen and oxygen molecules. Water vapor becomes part of the air. When water becomes part of the air, it is no longer liquid water.

Review Questions

1. **What is water vapor?**

2. **Where is water vapor?**

3. **What does water vapor look like?**

4. **What happens when a wet object gets dry?**

Evaporation

Evaporation is the change from liquid to gas. In the case of water, liquid water changes into water vapor. The water vapor then moves into the air. But what actually happens when evaporation takes place? To find out, we have to think about water as molecules.

A water molecule is made of three **atoms,** two hydrogen atoms and one oxygen atom. Scientists have figured out that one water molecule looks like this.

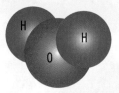

A representation of one water molecule

When water is in its liquid state, the molecules are all attracted to one another and in contact with each other. But they are not attached together tightly. As a result, the molecules move around and over one another. The molecules are in constant motion. That is why liquid water flows.

If you could see the molecules in a tiny spot of liquid water, they would look something like this.

A representation of many water molecules

Remember, the molecules are in constant motion. They are bumping into each other all the time. Sometimes a water molecule at the surface gets bumped so hard that it is knocked free from the mass of liquid. The free molecule moves into the air as a water-vapor molecule.

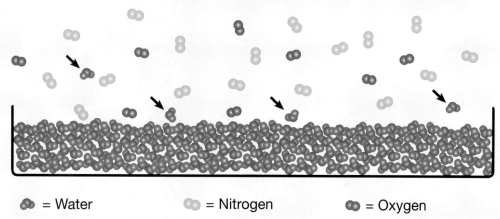

&ball; = Water   &ball; = Nitrogen   &ball; = Oxygen

Water molecules go into the air, which is mostly nitrogen and oxygen molecules.

Adding Heat

The rate at which water molecules escape from the liquid depends on how hard the water molecules hit each other. One way to increase the force with which molecules hit each other is to heat them up. When water is heated, the molecules move faster. When fast-moving molecules hit each other, they hit each other harder. As a result, more molecules break free from the surface of hot water than from cold water.

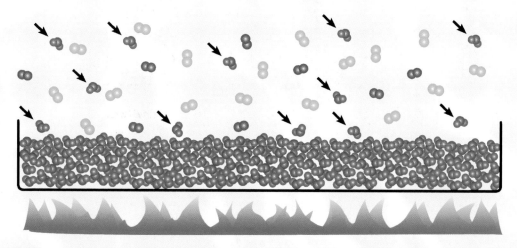

Water evaporates faster when water is heated.

There is a limit to the amount of water vapor that can enter the air. When the air has taken in as much water vapor as it can, the air is **saturated** with water vapor. Cold air can hold only a small amount of water vapor. It doesn't take much evaporated water to saturate cold air.

Warm air is different. Warm air can take in a lot of water vapor before it is saturated. But there is still a limit to the amount of water vapor that warm air can hold.

There are two general rules about evaporation.

1. The warmer the water, the faster it evaporates.

2. The warmer the air, the more water vapor it can hold.

Review Questions

1. **What causes evaporation?**

2. **Why does warm water evaporate faster than cold water?**

3. **How is water vapor different from liquid water?**

4. **How does temperature affect the amount of water vapor in the air?**

Surface-Area Experiment

Julie and Art wanted to find out how **surface area** affects evaporation. They decided to do an experiment. They had some plastic boxes to put water in, some graph paper, and a set of measuring tools. They were ready to start.

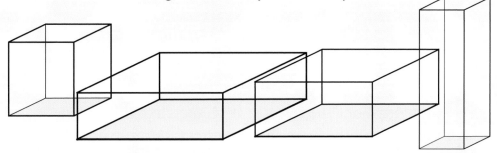

Julie had an idea for measuring the surface area of each box. She traced around each box on the graph paper. She used the meter tape to measure the distance between the lines on the graph paper. The lines were 1 centimeter (cm) apart.

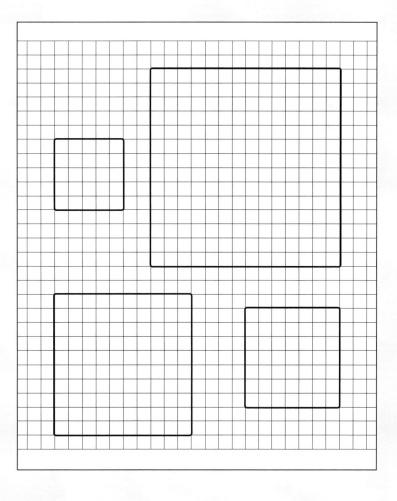

31

The two students numbered the boxes. The box with the smallest surface area was number 1. Then they measured 50 milliliters (mL) of water into each box. They placed the four boxes on the counter by a window.

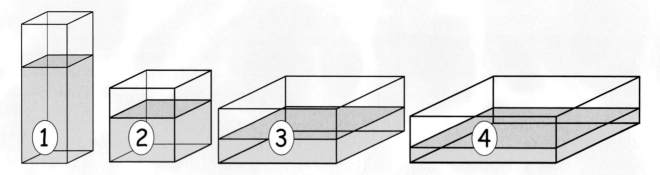

One week later Julie and Art measured the amount of water in each box. Box 1 had 46 mL. Box 2 had 42 mL. Box 3 had 34 mL. Box 4 had 18 mL.

Art thought about the results. It seemed like the surface area of the water in the boxes had an effect on the evaporation. But he wasn't sure. Julie suggested organizing the results of the experiment. The students decided to do the following.

- Make a T-table to display their data.

- Make a graph of their data.

- Describe what they learned from the experiment.

Can you help Julie and Art? Use the information they gathered to write a report about the effect of surface area on evaporation. Be sure to include the three kinds of information listed above.

Review Questions

1. **What was the independent variable in Julie and Art's experiment?**

2. **What was the dependent variable in their experiment?**

3. **What variables did they control?**

4. **What additional information would be useful to better understand how surface area affects evaporation?**

Condensation

When water evaporates, where does it go? It goes into the air. Water is always evaporating. Clothes are drying on clotheslines. Wet streets are drying after a rain. Water is evaporating from lakes and oceans all the time. Every day more than 1,000 cubic kilometers (km^3) of water evaporates worldwide. And all that water vapor goes into the air! That's nearly 240 cubic miles of water. That amount of water would cover the entire state of California 3 meters (10 feet) deep.

What happens to all that water in the air? As long as the air stays warm, the water stays in the air as water vapor. Warmth (heat) is energy. As long as the molecules of water vapor have a lot of energy in the form of heat, they continue to exist as gas.

But if the air cools, things change. As the air cools, all the molecules lose energy and slow down. This is when molecules of water vapor start to come together. Slowing down and coming together is called **condensation.** Condensation is the change from gas to liquid.

Molecules of condensed water vapor form tiny masses of liquid water. When invisible water vapor in the atmosphere condenses, the water becomes visible again. **Clouds** and **fog** are made of these tiniest masses of liquid water.

Condensation usually happens on a cold surface. In class you observed condensation on the cold surface of a plastic cup filled with ice water. But there are no cups of ice water in the sky. What kind of surface does water vapor condense on?

Most condensation in the air starts with dust particles. Water molecules attach to a dust particle. When a tiny mass of water has formed on a dust particle, other water molecules will join the liquid mass.

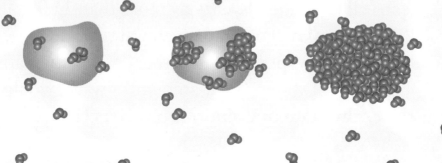

The mass grows and grows until a tiny droplet of water has formed.

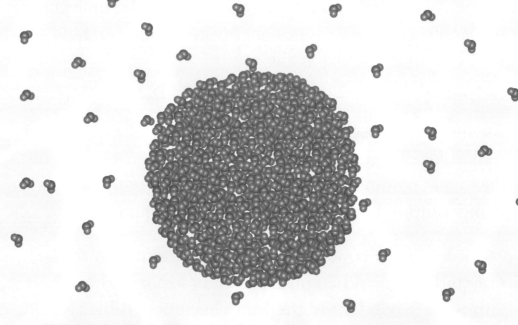

When you look up in the sky and see clouds, you are seeing droplets of liquid water. Each droplet is made up of billions of water molecules, but a single droplet is still too small to see. But you can see them when trillions and trillions of them are close together in clouds.

Where else have you seen condensation besides up in the sky in the form of clouds? Sometimes water vapor condenses close to the ground. This is called fog. Being in fog is really being in a cloud that is at ground level.

Fog close to the ground

As you know, water vapor doesn't always condense in air. If you go out early in the morning following a warm day, you might see condensation called **dew.** In the pictures below, dew formed on a spider web and along the edges of the leaves on a plant.

Dew on a spider web

Dew on plant leaves

Condensation on a window

Water vapor condenses indoors, too. On a cold morning you might see condensation on your kitchen window. Or if you go outside into the cold wearing your glasses, they could get fogged with condensation when you go back inside.

What happens to the bathroom mirror after you take a shower? The air in the bathroom is warm and saturated with water vapor. When the air makes contact with the cool mirror, the water vapor condenses on the smooth surface. That's why the mirror is foggy and wet.

Condensation on glasses

Condensation on the mirror

When the temperature drops below the **freezing point** of water (0°C or 32°F), water vapor will condense and freeze. Frozen condensation is called **frost.** Frost is tiny crystals of ice. Frost might form on a car window on a cold night. You can also see frost on plants early on a winter morning. But you have to get up before the Sun if you want to see the beautiful frost patterns.

Frost on a window

Frost on plants

Review Questions

1. **What is condensation?**

2. **What role does temperature play in condensation?**

3. **What is frost?**

4. **Why does condensation form on a glass of iced tea?**

Summary: Water Vapor

Water is a unique substance. It exists on Earth in all three common states of matter, solid, liquid, and gas. The solid state is called ice. The liquid state is called liquid water, or just water. The gas state is called **water vapor.**

Water changes between the gas and liquid states easily. When liquid water changes to water vapor, we say the water dried up. When we describe the change from liquid to gas scientifically, we say the water **evaporated.**

When liquid water appears out of thin air, we have several common names for it. The name we use depends on when and where the water appears. When it appears as tiny droplets in the air, we call it **clouds** and **fog.** When it appears on windows, plants, and cars, we call it **dew.** The scientific name for water that appears out of the air is **condensation.**

What causes water to evaporate and condense? Energy in the form of heat.

When you put a pan of water on the stove, heat energy transfers to the **water molecules.** The water molecules move faster and bang into one another harder. Molecules at the surface of the water get knocked free. The free molecules enter the air as water vapor. The larger the **surface area** of water exposed to air, the faster the water evaporates.

The mixture of gases we call air is all free molecules. Most of the air molecules are nitrogen and oxygen. Water molecules are a small but important part of the air. Water vapor will never be a large part of the air because there is a limit to the amount of water the air can hold. When air is holding all the water vapor it can, the air is **saturated.**

Warm air can hold more water vapor than cold air. This is a very important idea. Think about a mass of warm air that is saturated with water vapor. What will happen if the mass of warm, saturated air cools down? Cool air can't hold as much water as warm air. What will happen to the water in the air?

When water vapor cools, molecules move slower. Slower water molecules start to stick together. Water molecules in contact with one another condense to form liquid water.

Condensation usually starts on a surface of some kind. It could be a window or a plant. Or it could be a tiny bit of dust floating around in the air. Once a few molecules of water have condensed on a surface, other molecules will condense on the tiny spot of liquid water. The spot of water will grow until it is big enough to see. Visible condensation is known as clouds, fog, and dew.

Fog and low clouds over South San Francisco, California

When the temperature is below freezing (0°C or 32°F), you might see **frost** in the early morning. Frost is frozen condensation. It can form on windows, cars, and outdoor plants. Frost is made of tiny crystals of ice. The patterns created by the crystals in frost can be very beautiful. But to see them you have to get up early. As soon as sunshine falls on the frost, it will melt. If you get up late, all you will see is dew.

Summary Questions

Now is a good time to review what you have recorded in your science notebook. Think about the evaporation and condensation investigations you conducted.

1. What happens when liquid water evaporates?

2. What happens when water vapor condenses?

3. What is frost and how does it form?

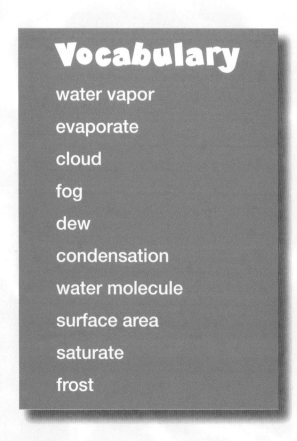

Vocabulary

water vapor

evaporate

cloud

fog

dew

condensation

water molecule

surface area

saturate

frost

Extensions

Math Problem of the Week

Some students set up an investigation to find out what effect surface area has on the rate of evaporation. They used a cake pan, a water glass, a cottage-cheese container, and an olive jar. The students put 100 mL of water in each container. They measured the water remaining in each container on days 2, 4, and 6.

Container	Water remaining on		
	Day 2	Day 4	Day 6
Cake pan	75 mL	50 mL	25 mL
Water glass	90 mL	80 mL	70 mL
Cottage-cheese	80 mL	60 mL	40 mL
Olive jar	95 mL	90 mL	85 mL

1. In which container will all the water evaporate first? On which day will that happen?

2. In which container will all the water evaporate last? On which day will that happen?

Home/School Connection

How fast does water evaporate in your home? Set up an evaporation gizmo to find out.

You will need

1 Plastic soda straw

3 Paper clips

1 Piece of string

2 Zip bags, same size

2 Paper towels

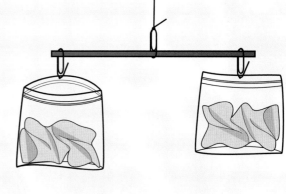

Moisten the paper towels. Put one in each bag. Seal one bag and leave the other open. Balance the system. Observe.

Where did the water go? The amount of water vapor in the air is called **humidity.** When air contains as much water vapor as it can possibly hold, the humidity is 100%. How could the humidity of the air affect the rate of evaporation?

Uneven Heating

Stars are huge energy generators. Energy shines out from them in all directions. Most of this energy streams out into space and never hits anything. A small amount, however, hits objects in the universe. When you look into the sky on a dark, clear night, you see thousands of stars. You see them because a tiny amount of energy from the stars goes into your eye.

During the day, you are aware of the energy coming from a much closer star, the Sun. The most important forms of energy coming from the Sun are heat and light. When heat and light come to Earth, you can feel the heat and see the light. Heat and light from the Sun are called **solar energy.**

When light from the Sun hits matter, such as Earth's surface, two things can happen. The light can be **reflected** or absorbed by the matter. If the light is reflected, it simply bounces off the matter and continues in a new direction. But if the light is absorbed, the matter gains energy. Usually the added energy is in the form of heat. When matter absorbs energy, its temperature goes up.

Sunset over a bay in Baja California

Heating It Up

The amount of solar energy coming from the Sun is pretty uniform. But the temperature of Earth's surface is not uniform. Some locations get warmer than other locations. Why is that?

There are several variables that affect how hot a material will get when solar energy shines on it. The table below lists several variables and how each affects the temperature change of a material.

Variable	Effect
Length of exposure	Longer exposure = higher temperature
Intensity of solar energy	Greater intensity = higher temperature
Color of material	Darker color = higher temperature
Properties of material	Water shows the least temperature change

Length of exposure is how long the Sun shines on an object.

Intensity of solar energy is how concentrated the energy is. If the light has to shine through clouds, for instance, the intensity will be reduced. Clouds reflect and absorb some of the energy before it gets to Earth's surface. The brighter the sunshine falling on an object, the warmer the object will be.

Color is important because different colors absorb solar energy differently. Black absorbs the most solar energy. White absorbs the least solar energy.

The **chemical properties** of materials affect how hot they get when they absorb solar energy. As you found out in your experiments, a volume of soil gets a lot hotter than an equal volume of water when they are put side by side in the sunshine. Water heats up slowly and soil heats up rapidly when they get the same amount of energy. Water cools slowly and soil cools rapidly when they are moved to the shade.

Solar Energy in Action

Think about a summer trip to the beach. On a cloudless day the Sun shines down with equal intensity on the town of San Clemente, California, the sandy beach, and the ocean. It's a hot day.

When the car stops in the parking lot in the early afternoon, the parking lot is hot. The black asphalt has absorbed a lot of solar energy, and its temperature is 50°C (120°F)! You are anxious to get to the beach. You dash across the hot parking lot and onto the white sand. Whew! The white sand isn't as hot. It is a bearable 32°C (90°F). You keep going, right into the water. You finally get relief from the intense southern California heat. The temperature of the ocean water is 22°C (72°F).

The asphalt, sand, and seawater were all subjected to the same intensity of solar energy for the same length of time. But they are all different temperatures.

Black asphalt absorbs a lot of energy and gets very hot. White sand reflects a lot of solar energy. Sand doesn't get as hot as asphalt. Water absorbs a lot of energy, but it stays cool.

The temperature of Earth's surface is not the same everywhere. Land gets hotter than water in the sunshine. Land gets colder than water when the Sun goes down. Land heats up and cools off rapidly. Water heats up and cools off slowly. The result is **uneven heating** of Earth's surface.

Uneven Heating Worldwide

You can experience uneven heating of Earth's surface with your bare feet during a trip to the beach. The difference in temperature between the asphalt and water is obvious. On a larger scale, the whole planet is heated unevenly. The tropics (near the equator) are warmer. The polar areas are cooler. That's because the intensity of the solar energy is greater in the tropics.

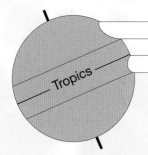

A beam of sunlight spreads over a larger area toward the poles.

The illustration shows how sunshine comes straight down on the tropics. But the sunshine comes at an angle toward the poles. You can see how the same amount of light is spread over a much larger area in the north than in the tropics. This results in uneven heating between the tropics and the polar areas.

Review Questions

1. **What causes Earth's surface to heat up?**

2. **What are some of the variables that cause uneven heating of Earth's surface?**

3. **What happens to the temperature of equal volumes of soil and water when they are placed in the sunshine for 30 minutes?**

Wind!

Kite flying can be a lot of fun if the conditions are right. If the conditions are wrong, kite flying can be a drag. What makes conditions right for kite flying? **Wind.**

Wind is air in motion. Air is matter. Air has mass and takes up space. When a mass of air is in motion, it can move things around. Wind can blow leaves down the street, lift your hat off your head, and carry a kite into the air.

Sometimes air is still. Other times the wind is blowing. What causes the wind to blow? What puts the air into motion? The answer is energy. It takes energy to move air. The energy to create wind comes from the Sun.

Wind lifts a kite into the air.

Air is molecules of oxygen and nitrogen (and a few other gases). The molecules are flying around and banging into each other, the land, and the sea. Let's imagine we are back at the beach at San Clemente. It's early morning. The air over the land and the air over the sea are both the same cool temperature.

Air (molecules)

Sea

Land

In early morning, the land, sea, and air are all the same cool temperature.

46

As the Sun shines down on the land and sea, solar energy is absorbed. The land heats up quickly. The sea heats up very slowly. By noon the land is hot, but the sea is still cool. Earth's surface is heated unevenly. The afternoon wind starts. Here's why.

When air molecules bang into the hot surface of the land, energy transfers to the air molecules. Because of this **energy transfer,** the air molecules fly around faster. The air gets hot. The hot-air molecules bang into each other harder. That pushes the molecules farther apart.

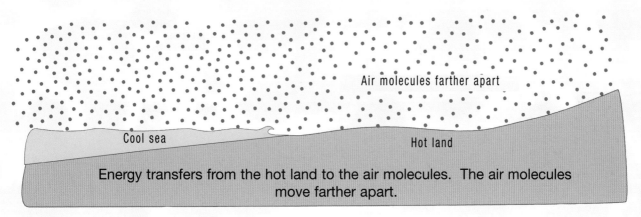

Energy transfers from the hot land to the air molecules. The air molecules move farther apart.

Over the ocean, air molecules are banging into the cool surface of the water. The air stays cool. The air molecules continue to move at a slower speed. The cool-air molecules don't hit each other as hard, so they stay closer together.

A cubic meter of hot air has fewer molecules than a cubic meter of cool air. The hot air is less dense than an equal volume of cool air.

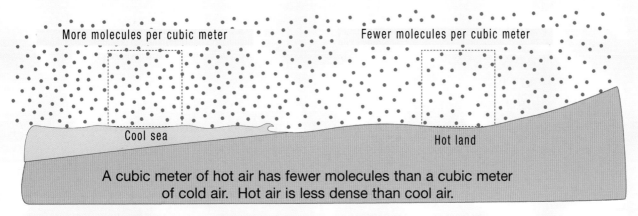

A cubic meter of hot air has fewer molecules than a cubic meter of cold air. Hot air is less dense than cool air.

The Wind Starts

You know that cork floats on water. Cork floats on water because it is less dense than water. If you take a cork to the bottom of the sea and let it go, it will float to the surface.

That's exactly what happens with warm and cold air. The warm air over the land floats upward because it is less dense than the cool air over the sea. The denser, cool air flows into the area where the light, warm air is and pushes it upward. The movement of denser air from the sea to the warm land is wind. Wind is the movement of denser air to an area where the air is less dense.

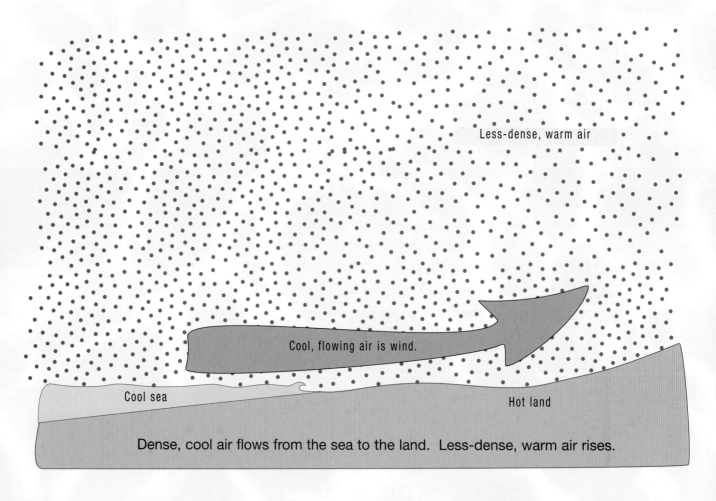

Less-dense, warm air

Cool, flowing air is wind.

Cool sea

Hot land

Dense, cool air flows from the sea to the land. Less-dense, warm air rises.

There is more to the story of wind. Two things happen at the same time to create wind. The warm air cools as it rises, becoming denser than the surrounding air. At the same time, the dense air from the sea warms up as it flows over the hot land.

48

As a result, air starts to move in a big circle. Air that is warmed by the hot land moves upward. The warm air cools as it moves up, gets denser, and starts to fall. The rising and falling air sets up a big circular air current. The circular current is called a **convection current.**

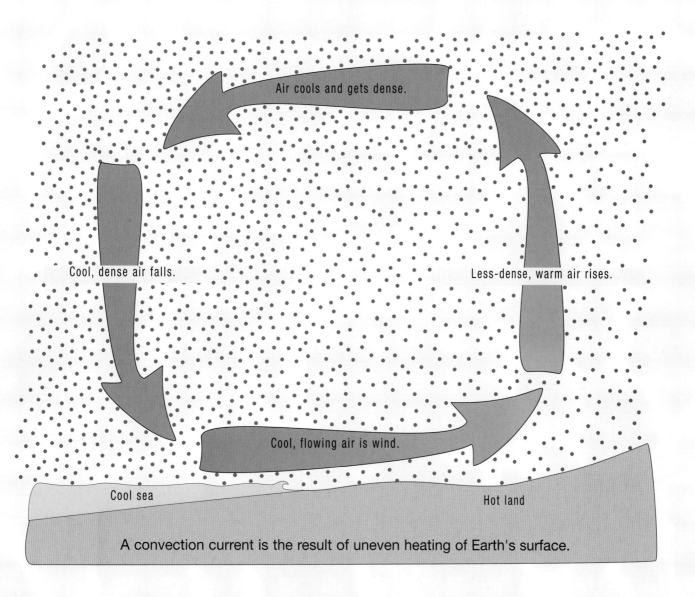

Air cools and gets dense.

Cool, dense air falls.

Less-dense, warm air rises.

Cool, flowing air is wind.

Cool sea

Hot land

A convection current is the result of uneven heating of Earth's surface.

As long as Earth's surface continues to be heated unevenly, the convection current will continue to flow. The part of the convection current that flows across Earth's surface is what we experience as wind. But what happens at night?

The Wind Changes Direction

When the Sun goes down, solar energy no longer falls on the land and sea. The land cools rapidly, but the sea stays at about the same temperature. The air over the cool land is no longer heated. The density of the air over land and sea is the same. The convection current stops flowing. The wind stops blowing.

What will happen if the night is really cold? The land will get cold. The air over the land will get cold. The cold air will become denser than the air over the sea. The denser air will flow from the land to the sea. The convection current will flow in the opposite direction, and the wind will blow from the land to the sea.

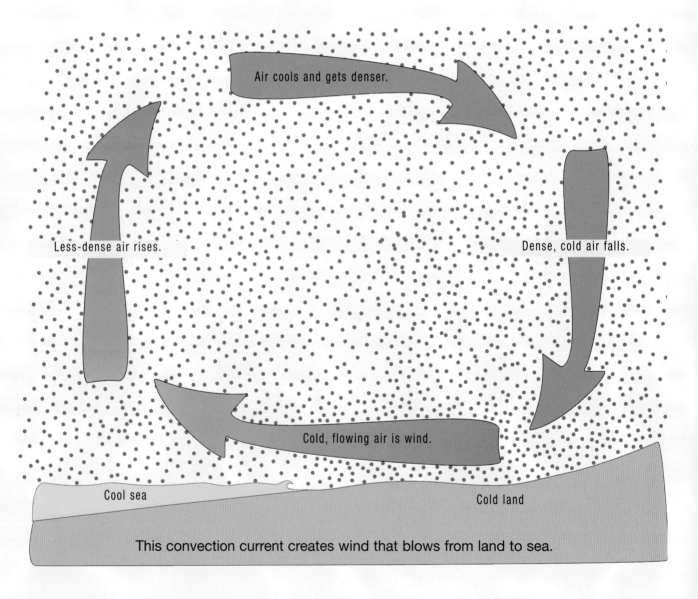

Air cools and gets denser.

Less-dense air rises.

Dense, cold air falls.

Cold, flowing air is wind.

Cool sea

Cold land

This convection current creates wind that blows from land to sea.

Convection Summary

Uneven heating of Earth's surface by the Sun causes uneven heating of the air over Earth's surface. Warm air is less dense than cold air. Cold, dense air flows to an area where the air is warmer and less dense. The less-dense air is pushed upward. As the warm air moves upward, it cools. Cool air is denser, so it falls back to Earth. This circular pattern of air flow is a convection current.

Convection currents produce wind. The greater the difference in temperature between the warm and cold air masses, the harder and faster the wind will blow. Uneven heating of Earth's surface is the cause of many weather changes on Earth, including hurricanes, tornadoes, and thunderstorms.

Review Questions

1. **Explain how convection currents are produced in the air.**

2. **Explain what causes wind.**

3. **Describe what happens to air molecules when air is heated.**

4. **What is the source of energy that causes the wind to blow?**

The Pressure Is On!

Earth is surrounded by air. The air reaches up about 500 kilometers (300 miles) above Earth's surface. The whole layer of air covering the Earth is the **atmosphere.**

Air has mass. How much? Imagine putting a 1-cm square of paper on the ground. Then think about a column of air 1 centimeter square from the ground all the way up to the top of the atmosphere. The mass of the air resting on that piece of paper would be about 1.2 kilograms (2.6 pounds).

The top of your head has a surface area of about 150 square centimeters. That means every time you stand under the open sky, you have the pressure of 180 kilograms (400 pounds) of air pushing down on the top of your head. That's like wearing a hat with a refrigerator on it! Is it safe to go outdoors?

Don't worry, it's safe. The force caused by the mass of the air above you is called **atmospheric pressure.** Your body can easily push back with a force equal to the atmospheric pressure. You are usually not aware of the pressure at all. But sometimes you are. Have you ever felt your ears "pop"? That sometimes happens when you are riding down a long hill in a car. What causes that?

Atmospheric Pressure

Air is made of molecules. Molecules have mass. If you pile a lot of molecules on top of each other, the load gets heavier and heavier. That's what the atmosphere is, a huge pile of air molecules.

Imagine molecules as big as watermelons. A big melon is pretty heavy. It might have a mass of 10 kilograms. If you place the melon on a scale, the scale will read 10 kg.

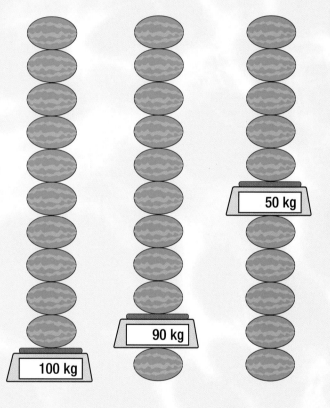

Think about a stack of 10 watermelons. The scale would now read 100 kg. The mass on the scale is equal to the sum of the 10 melons.

But the pressure is not the same on all the melons. This can be seen by moving the scale from the bottom of the stack of melons to someplace else in the stack. If the scale is moved between melon 1 and melon 2, the mass on the scale is 90 kg. Between melons 5 and 6, the scale reads 50 kg.

Air molecules are tiny, but they stack up the same way. A pressure gauge at Earth's surface will show the pressure that results from a stack of molecules 500 kilometers deep. The pressure is greatest at Earth's surface. This is just like the pressure on the watermelon at the bottom of the stack is greatest.

If you could see air molecules, you would see that they are compressed near Earth's surface. Because the molecules are close together, air is densest near Earth's surface. Denser air has more molecules per unit of volume.

Let's imagine that a small vial contains 100 air molecules at Earth's surface.

Vial of 100 air molecules

As you look higher in the atmosphere, you see that the molecules get farther apart. Air higher in the atmosphere is not compressed as much. The air is less dense. The same vial might contain only 50 molecules because the air is less compressed. The molecules are farther apart.

Vial of 50 air molecules

Below is a mountain in the atmosphere. At sea level, the air is dense and the pressure is high. Going up to the top of a tall mountain, like Mt. Whitney in the Sierra Nevada, is like climbing a ladder 4.4 km (2.75 miles) into the air. Up on the mountain, 4.4 kilometers of air is below you. This air is not applying pressure on you. The small mass of air above you does not push with as much pressure, so the air is less dense. That means there are fewer molecules in the vial.

The atmosphere is densest at sea level. The atmosphere gets less and less dense as you rise higher above sea level. As the density of air goes down, so does the atmospheric pressure.

The Effects of Atmospheric Pressure

Atmospheric pressure changes with **elevation.** As you go higher in the atmosphere, the pressure gets lower. Air pushes with less force in the mountains than it does at sea level.

Pressure is a result of air molecules banging into each other and objects. Pressure goes up when *more* molecules are banging into things. This happens when air gets compressed. Pressure goes up when molecules bang into things *harder.* This happens when air gets hot. Because air molecules are flying in all directions, pressure acts in all directions equally.

In class you worked with syringes connected with a tube. When you pulled one plunger out, the other one went in. Why?

Here's a drawing showing two syringes. The density of air molecules inside and outside the syringes is the same.

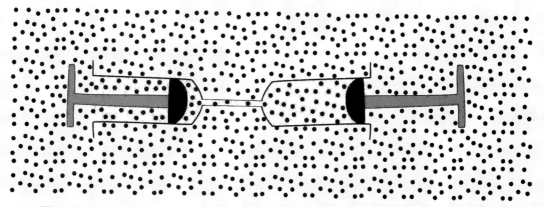

The density of air molecules is the same inside and outside the syringes.

When both plungers are pulled out and held, the number of molecules inside the syringes does not change. But the space they are in gets bigger. The molecules fill the larger space evenly.

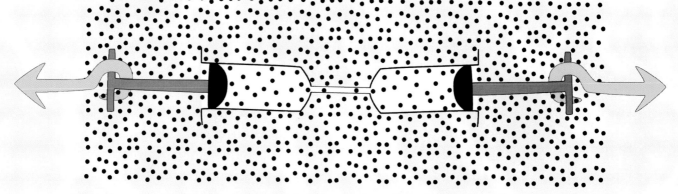

The space inside the two syringes is bigger when the plunger is pulled out. The molecules inside the syringes fill the space, so the density is lower.

The density of molecules inside the syringes is lower than the density of molecules outside. That means the air pressure inside the syringes (blue arrows) is lower than the atmospheric pressure outside (red arrows).

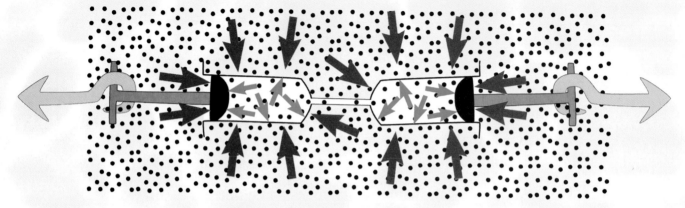

Pressure outside the syringes is greater than pressure inside the syringes.

When the plunger on the right is released, the stronger pressure outside pushes it in until the density of molecules inside the syringes is the same as the density of molecules outside the syringes. When the density is the same, the pressure is the same. The plunger stops moving.

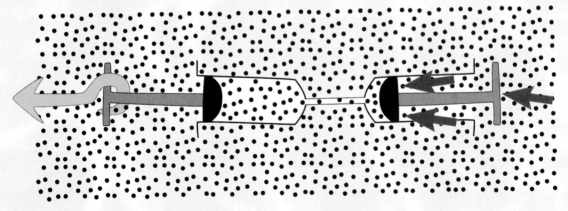

Atmospheric pressure pushes the plunger in until the density of air molecules inside the syringes is equal to the density of molecules outside.

It is important to understand that pulling the plunger out on one syringe does not *suck* the plunger into the other syringe. The right way to think about the event is that pulling out one plunger reduces the pressure inside both syringes. Atmospheric pressure then *pushes* the plunger until the inside and outside pressure are the same.

Atmospheric Pressure and Weather

Meteorologists are scientists who study **weather.** By studying atmospheric pressure, temperature, and humidity, they can predict what the weather will be in a few days or a few weeks. Predicting weather is called **forecasting.**

You have probably heard **weather forecasts** on TV. Often the weather forecasters will mention high pressure or low pressure. They are referring to the atmospheric pressure. Different areas of Earth's surface have slightly different atmospheric temperatures. This can be the result of uneven heating.

Hot air expands, becomes less dense, and exerts less pressure. That makes a local low-pressure area. Cold air contracts, becomes denser, and exerts more pressure. That makes a local high-pressure area. If there is a cooler, high-pressure area near a warm, low-pressure area, the difference in pressure will start a convection current. And that means wind. That's one kind of weather forecast a meteorologist can make.

Review Questions

1. **What is atmospheric pressure and what causes it?**

2. **Is atmospheric pressure higher on a mountaintop or at sea level? Explain why.**

3. **Rudy's family drove from San Francisco to Tioga Pass in Yosemite National Park. The pass is over 3,000 meters high. A bag of chips they had for snacks was puffed up like a pillow when they got to the pass. Why?**

4. **Rudy finished a plastic bottle of spring water on the pass. He put the lid on the empty bottle tightly. When he got back home in San Francisco, the bottle was crushed. Why?**

Summary: Heating Earth

Energy from the Sun in the form of heat and light falls on Earth during the day. Materials on Earth's surface absorb the **solar energy** and get warm. Some materials, such as rock and soil, heat up quickly when they absorb energy. Other materials, such as water, heat up slowly when they absorb energy. The result is **uneven heating** of Earth's surface. The land changes temperature quickly. The oceans change temperature slowly.

Air is a mixture of gas molecules. Most of the molecules are nitrogen and oxygen. Air molecules are flying around all the time. When air molecules bang into Earth's surface, they can gain or lose energy. Gain or loss of energy is **energy transfer.**

On a sunny day, the land gets hot. Air molecules that bang into the land gain energy. Those molecules move faster.

When air molecules bang into a cold surface, such as the ocean, they lose energy. Those molecules move slower.

Molecule Energy and Gas Density

Fast-moving molecules bang into each other harder. When molecules hit hard, they push each other farther apart. When molecules are farther apart, the mass of air is less dense. Slow-moving molecules hit each other with less force. They move closer together. The air becomes denser. As a result of energy transfer, warm air is less dense than cold air.

Convection Currents and Wind

Often uneven heating of Earth's surface results in masses of air of different temperatures. A mass of warm air over the land will be less dense than a mass of cold air over the ocean. When this happens, the cool, dense air will push the warm, less-dense air upward. As the cold air flows onshore, it is warmed by the land. The new warm air is pushed up by more cold air from the sea.

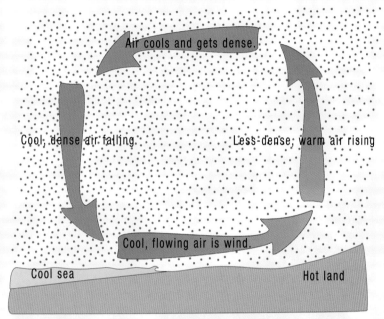

Air cools and gets dense.

Cool, dense air falling.

Less-dense, warm air rising

Cool, flowing air is wind.

Cool sea

Hot land

A convection current is the result of uneven heating of Earth's surface.

As the warm air rises, it cools. When the mass of air cools, it becomes dense and falls back to Earth's surface. The cool, dense air will once again flow onshore.

The circular flow of air is a **convection current.** The part of the convection current where cool air from the sea flows onshore creates **wind.** This is how convection currents produce wind all over Earth.

Atmospheric Pressure

Air molecules have mass. The air molecules stacked up from Earth's surface to the top of the **atmosphere** have a lot of mass. All those molecules push on Earth's surface with a lot of pressure. Because the pressure in the air pushes *in all directions,* air pressure is pushing equally on every side of every object that is in the air.

The pressure exerted by the air is called **atmospheric pressure.** Atmospheric pressure is pushing on all sides of you, as well as your desk, books, school, and town.

Atmospheric pressure is the result of the force applied by the air above you. If you go higher in the atmosphere, to the top of a tall mountain, the atmospheric pressure will be less. When you look down from the mountain, you can see that there is a lot of air below you. That air is not above you, it is below you. Atmospheric pressure is produced by the mass of air above you. Less air above results in less pressure.

The atmosphere is densest at sea level. The atmosphere gets less and less dense as you rise higher above sea level. As the density of air goes down, so does the atmospheric pressure.

When there is less atmospheric pressure, the air molecules are not pushed as close together. The air at the top of a mountain is less dense. When people talk about "thin air," they are really talking about air that is less dense.

Meteorologists are scientists who study **weather.** Differences in atmospheric pressure cause changes in the weather. By measuring the pressure at different places on Earth, meteorologists can make better **weather forecasts.**

Summary Questions

Now is a good time to review what you have recorded in your science notebook. Think about the uneven heating and convection investigations you conducted.

1. What causes uneven heating of Earth's surface?

2. Explain how uneven heating of Earth's surface results in convection currents.

3. What is atmospheric pressure and what causes it?

4. In what direction does atmospheric pressure push?

Vocabulary

solar energy

uneven heating

energy transfer

convection current

wind

atmosphere

atmospheric pressure

meteorologist

weather

weather forecast

Extensions

Math Problem of the Week

Four students had questions about how earth materials heat up in the sunshine.

1. How does length of exposure to sunshine affect final temperature?
2. How does surface area affect the length of time it takes to raise the temperature 10°C?
3. How does the volume of material in the container affect heating?
4. What kind of material heats up fastest in the sunshine?

Each student designed an experiment. The students worked with these variables.

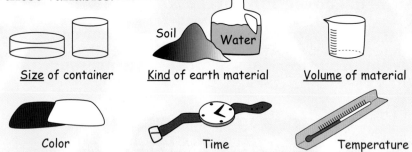

Size of container   Kind of earth material   Volume of material

Color   Time   Temperature

Identify the independent, dependent, and controlled variables in each experiment.

Experiment	Independent variable	Dependent variable	Controlled variables
1	Time	Temperature	Size, kind, volume, color
2			
3			
4			

Home/School Connection

Look at seed packets or seed catalogs to find out how many days it takes for some of your favorite vegetables to bear fruit. Count each day as a "sun day" and compare the results for different plants.

Where Is Earth's Water?

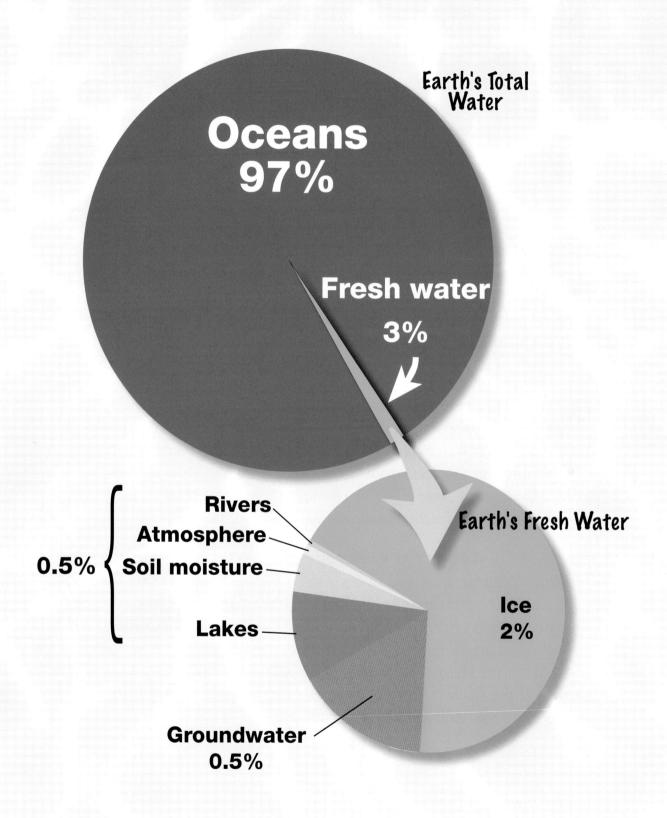

Earth's Total Water

Oceans 97%

Fresh water 3%

Earth's Fresh Water

Rivers

Atmosphere

Soil moisture

0.5%

Lakes

Ice 2%

Groundwater 0.5%

Earth's Water

Earth is known as the water planet. Earth is the only planet that has vast oceans of water. Seventy-one percent of Earth's surface is covered by water. If your first view of Earth from space was of the Pacific Ocean, you might think Earth was completely covered in water.

Where Is Earth's Water?

Water is almost everywhere on Earth. It's in the oceans, in and on the land, and in the atmosphere. The pie charts on the previous page show how Earth's water is distributed. Just about all of Earth's water is in the oceans. Ocean water is **salt water.** Land plants and animals, including humans, cannot use salt water. So 97% of Earth's water is not good for people to drink.

To survive, humans need some of the 3% of the water without salt called **fresh water.** After subtracting the frozen water, about 1% of Earth's water remains. This fresh water is in lakes, rivers, groundwater, soil, the atmosphere, and organisms. It is known as free water because it is free to move around the planet. Free water is being refreshed and recycled all the time.

Most of the water we can easily use comes from rivers and lakes. Water in lakes and rivers is known as **surface water.** Water that falls as **precipitation** can either remain as surface water or seep underground where it is stored in soil or porous rock. Underground water is known as groundwater. You can see from the pie chart that there is more water stored underground than at the surface. Groundwater is close at hand, but we can't see it. People drill wells to get groundwater.

Water Use

Americans place high demands on water sources. Think about this. In 1995 people in the United States used about 1,204 billion liters (319 billion gallons) of surface water every day. They also used about 289 billion liters (77 billion gallons) of groundwater every day. That's a total of nearly 1,500 billion liters every day. That works out to about 5,450 liters (1,440 gallons) of water every day for every person in the country!

Of course, you don't use 5,450 liters yourself. But water is needed to grow and prepare food, to make products like paper and cloth, and for hundreds of other uses that benefit you.

People use water in many different ways. Most important, water is essential for life. Without water to drink we wouldn't survive. You can probably think of many nonessential ways you use water at home. You wash your clothes, brush your teeth, and cook your food with water. Swimming pools are filled with water and lawns are watered. Humans also use water for navigation through lakes and rivers, for creating electricity, in manufacturing, and for agriculture. All these activities require a lot of water. No additional water is coming to Earth. And the demand for water continues to grow. How will we survive?

We can't increase the amount of water on Earth. But we can make smart decisions about how much water we remove from natural systems. We can decide how the water is distributed, how it is used, and what happens to it after we use it. As the demand for water increases worldwide due to population increase, everyone will have to **conserve** water.

In California, about 75% of the free water is used for irrigating crops. We can save a lot of water by developing better ways to water crops.

Industry uses a lot of water to make things. Our water supply can be extended by finding ways to reuse and recycle water. Industry must also be careful not to let pollutants get into water supplies.

In the home, water-efficient toilets and washing machines can save a lot of water. Lawns and gardens should be watered at night to reduce water loss to evaporation. Gardens with native plants need little or no water at all. And keep water conservation in mind all the time. Every citizen will have to become more aware of the value of water and treat it as the most precious resource on Earth.

Review Questions

1. **Where is most of Earth's water?**

2. **What are the main sources of fresh water used by humans?**

3. **What can people do to make better use of the water that is available?**

The Water Cycle

Water molecules in the water you drink today may have once flowed down the Ohio River in the Midwest. Those same molecules may have washed one of Abraham Lincoln's shirts. They might even have been in a puddle lapped up by a thirsty saber-toothed cat!

A saber-toothed cat

Water is in constant motion on Earth. You can see water in motion in rushing streams and falling raindrops and snowflakes. But water is in motion in other places, too. Water is flowing slowly through the soil. Water is drifting across the sky in clouds. Water is rising through the roots and stems of plants. Water is in motion all over the world.

Think about the Ohio River for a moment. It flows all year long, year after year. Where does the water come from to keep the river flowing?

Ohio River

The water flowing in the river is renewed all the time. **Rain** and **snow** fall in the Ohio River Valley and the hills around it. The rain soaks into the soil and runs into the river. The snow melts in the spring and supplies water for the river during the summer. Rain and snow keep the Ohio River flowing.

The rain and snow in the Ohio River Valley are just a tiny part of a global system of water **recycling.** The global water recycling system is called the **water cycle.**

The big idea of the water cycle is this. Water evaporates from Earth's surface and goes into the atmosphere. Water in the atmosphere moves to a new location. The water then returns to Earth's surface in the new location. The new location gets a fresh supply of water.

A simple water-cycle diagram

Water Evaporates from Earth's Surface

The Sun drives the water cycle. Energy from the Sun falls on Earth's surface and changes liquid water into water vapor. The ocean is where most of the evaporation takes place. But water evaporates from lakes, rivers, soil, wet city streets, plants, animals, and wherever there is water. Water evaporates from all parts of Earth's surface, both water and land.

Water evaporates from all of Earth's surfaces.

Water vapor is made of individual water molecules. Water vapor enters the air and makes it moist. The moist air moves up in the atmosphere. As moist air rises, it cools. When water vapor cools, it condenses. Water in the atmosphere changes from gas to liquid. Tiny droplets of liquid water form. The condensed water is visible. We recognize condensed water as clouds, fog, and dew.

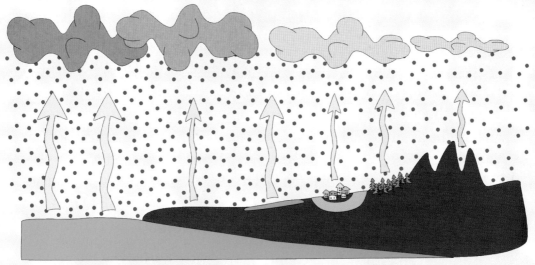

Water vapor condenses in the atmosphere to form clouds.

Water Falls Back to Earth's Surface

Wind blows clouds around. Clouds end up over mountains, forests, cities, deserts, and the ocean. When clouds are loaded with condensed water, the water falls back to Earth's surface as rain. If the temperature is really cold, the water will freeze and fall to Earth's surface as snow, **sleet,** or **hail.**

Water falls back to Earth's surface as rain, snow, sleet, and hail.

Water molecules move through the water cycle at different speeds. And they follow different paths. For example, rain may soak into the soil. A molecule might be taken in by plant roots. It might soon escape into the air through holes in plant leaves. If the air is cool, water might condense immediately as dew and fall back onto the soil. This is a very small water cycle that recycles water back to its starting place quickly.

Rain that lands on the roof of your school may flow to the ground. From there it could enter a stream. After a long journey, it could find its way to the ocean. There the rainwater could reenter the atmosphere as water vapor. By the time it condenses with millions of other molecules to form a drop, the rainwater could be hundreds of kilometers away from where it started. When the molecule returns to Earth's surface, it could fall on the roof of a school in another state. This is an example of a large water cycle that moves water to a new location.

Rain can sink into the ground or freeze in a **glacier.** A molecule far underground or deep in a mass of ice can take a long time to reenter the water cycle. It might take 100 years for a molecule of groundwater to come to the surface in a spring, and even longer for a molecule to break free from a glacier.

The Sun provides the energy to change water into vapor. Water vapor enters the air, where it is carried around the world. When water condenses, gravity pulls it back to Earth's surface. That's the water cycle, and it goes on endlessly.

Review Questions

1. **What is the water cycle?**

2. **When water falls from clouds, what forms can it take?**

3. **Describe a large water cycle that takes a long time to complete.**

4. **Describe a small water cycle that takes a short time to complete.**

Severe Weather

On August 29, 2005, **Hurricane** Katrina roared across the Gulf of Mexico and onto land. Throughout the country, people watched TV and listened to the radio as Katrina plowed into the states of Louisiana, Mississippi, and Alabama. The wind speed was 255 kilometers per hour (160 miles per hour). The rain poured down. When the storm had passed, hundreds of people were dead, hundreds of thousands were homeless, and the city of New Orleans was flooded.

Hurricane Katrina making landfall on the Gulf Coast, August 29, 2005

The cost of the damage was in the billions of dollars.

Weather is fairly predictable most of the time. During the summer months in San Francisco, mornings and afternoons are often foggy. There may be sunshine in the middle of the day. In the winter months, rain is common. In Los Angeles, hot, dry weather is typical in the summer. In Gulf states, summer days are often hot and humid (moist). In the Midwest and East, winters are usually cold, cloudy, and snowy. These are the normal weather conditions that people come to expect where they live.

It's the change from normal to the extreme that catches people's attention. **Tornadoes, thunderstorms,** windstorms, hurricanes, **drought,** and floods are examples of **severe weather.** Severe weather brings out-of-the-ordinary conditions. It may cause dangerous situations that can damage property and threaten lives.

What Is Weather?

We are surrounded by air. It's a little bit like living on the bottom of an ocean of air. Things are always going on in the air surrounding us. The condition of the air around us is what we call weather.

Weather can be described in terms of three important variables. They are heat, moisture, and movement. They are called variables because they change. A day with nice weather might be warm, but not too hot. The sky is clear with just a little bit of moisture in the air. The air is still or moving with a light breeze. That's a perfect day for most people. But not too many days are perfect. Usually it's too hot, too humid, too windy, or too something. But don't worry. Weather always changes.

What Causes Weather to Change?

Energy makes weather happen. Energy makes weather change. The source of energy to create and change weather is the Sun.

When sunshine is intense, the air gets hot. When sunshine is blocked by clouds, or when the Sun goes down, the air cools off.

Moisture in the air takes the form of humidity, clouds, and precipitation. Intense sunshine evaporates more water from Earth's surface. The result is more humidity, more cloud formation, and more rain. When sunshine is less intense, evaporation slows down.

Movement of air is wind. Uneven heating of Earth's surface results in uneven heating of the air touching Earth's surface. Warm air expands and gets less dense. Denser cool air flows under the warm air. This starts a convection current. The air flowing from the cool surface to the warm surface is wind.

Hurricanes and Tropical Storms

Hurricanes are wind systems that rotate around an eye, or center of low atmospheric pressure. Hurricanes form over warm tropical seas. They are classified on a scale from 1 to 5, with 5 being the most powerful storm. Katrina was category 4 as it approached the Gulf Coast of the United States.

Most hurricanes that hit the United States start as tropical storms in the Atlantic Ocean. They form during late summer and early fall when the ocean is warmest. As a tropical storm moves west, it draws energy from the warm water. The storm gets larger, and the wind spins faster and faster.

The spinning wind draws a lot of warm water vapor high in the storm system. When the vapor cools, it condenses. The process of condensation releases even more energy, which makes the system spin even faster. When the hurricane reaches land, the winds are blowing at deadly speeds, up to 250 km/h (155 mph). The rain is very heavy. The wind and rain can cause a lot of destruction.

As soon as a hurricane moves over land, it begins to lose strength. It no longer has warm water to pull energy and water vapor from. Within hours the wind and rain fall to safe levels.

Occasionally hurricanes form in the Pacific Ocean off the coast of Mexico. In 1997 ocean waters along the California coast were warmer than usual. Hurricane Linda formed near Mexico and headed north. Linda was the strongest storm ever recorded in the eastern Pacific, with winds estimated at 290 km/h (180 mph). Fortunately, the storm turned away from California.

Hurricane Linda near Baja California in 1997

Thunderstorms

Thunderstorms form when an air mass at the ground is much warmer and more humid than the air above. Rapid convection begins. As the warm, humid air rises, the water vapor in it condenses. The condensing water vapor releases more heat energy to the surrounding air, causing the air to rise even higher. The rapid movement of air also creates static electric charge on the clouds. When the static electricity discharges, lightning shoots from the clouds to the ground, and you hear the sound of rumbling thunder. Thunderstorms can cause death, start fires, and destroy communications systems. The powerful winds and heavy rain can cause property damage.

Thunderstorms are most common in the afternoon over land. The Sun heats Earth's surface and transfers heat to the air. When cold air flows under the warm air, thunderstorms are possible.

On the afternoon of July 30, 2003, a thunderstorm rolled across Edwards Air Force Base in the Mojave Desert of California. The storm was severe. It broke or uprooted hundreds of trees, damaged roofs of buildings, and caused power outages.

A massive thunderstorm rolling over Edwards AFB

A lightning strike at Edwards AFB

Tornadoes

Tornadoes are powerful forms of wind. They usually happen in late afternoons in spring or summer. When cold air over the land runs into a mass of warm air, the warm air is forced upward violently. At the same time, cooler, denser air flows in from the sides and twists the rising warm air. A spinning funnel forms that "sucks up" everything in its path like a giant vacuum cleaner. The air pressure inside the funnel is very low. The pressure outside the funnel is much higher. The extreme difference in air pressure can create wind speeds of 400 km/h (250 mph) or more. Tornadoes can seriously damage everything in their path.

A tornado rips through a small Texas town.

Tornadoes are most common in the south central part of the country, from Texas to Nebraska. Hundreds of tornadoes occur in this region each year. Warm, moist air from the Gulf of Mexico moves northward. It runs into cooler, drier air flowing down from Canada. This creates perfect conditions for tornadoes. That's why this part of the United States is called Tornado Alley.

Hot and Cold

Hot and cold weather are the direct result of solar energy. It gets hot when energy from the Sun is high. It gets cold when solar energy is low. The ocean also affects temperature. The highest and lowest temperatures are never close to the ocean. Water has the ability to absorb and release large amounts of energy without changing temperature much. This keeps places close to the ocean from getting really hot or cold.

Here is a table of temperature extremes for the United States and the world. These temperatures are deadly for most organisms. Only a few tough organisms are able to survive such temperatures.

Range	Location	High Temperature	Low Temperature
United States	Death Valley, California	57°C (134°F)	
	Prospect Creek, Alaska		−62°C (−80°F)
World	Al Aziziyah, Libya	58°C (136°F)	
	Vostok, Antarctica		−89°C (−128°F)

Western Weather Extremes

The west coast of North America does not have many hurricanes and tornadoes. But it does have weather extremes. Most of them involve the ocean.

During the winter, it typically rains and snows along the west coast and in the western mountains. When large storms come in from the Pacific Ocean, wind and rain can cause property damage and flooding. In the mountains, the precipitation comes down as snow. Intense snowstorms are called **blizzards.** A single blizzard can drop 4 meters (13 feet) or more of snow. The snow for a whole winter might exceed 10 meters (33 feet).

Meteorologists talk about a weather event called Pineapple Express. It's not a train, but a band of warm, moist air that flows to the west coast from the warm oceans around the Hawaiian Islands. When the warm, humid Pineapple Express meets cold air flowing down from Alaska, a violent winter storm can develop. High winds and heavy rain can uproot trees, destroy homes, and flood large areas of lowlands.

The Pineapple Express carries large amounts of moisture to California.

When seasonal rain and snow fail to develop, a different kind of severe weather can occur. Drought. Drought is less-than-normal precipitation. In the southwest, this means less rain in the deserts and hills, and less snow in the mountains. Less snow means less spring runoff. Less runoff results in reduced flow in rivers and streams. Lakes and ponds shrink and in some cases dry up completely. Soil moisture dries up and groundwater decreases. Reservoirs used to store water for human use shrink.

Droughts stress natural and human communities. Fish and other aquatic organisms may die. Plants that are not adapted for dry environments may die. Reduced water for crops means less food production. People have to conserve water by using less and recycling water when possible.

Serious droughts are not uncommon. During the early 1930s, parts of Colorado, Kansas, New Mexico, Oklahoma, and Texas received little rain. Crops failed. Then came the relentless winds. The farms in the area were stripped of their rich topsoil. The farmers had to leave the area because their fields were destroyed. Thousands of families had to leave the area known as the Dust Bowl.

This river stopped flowing during a drought.

Could it happen again? Many climate scientists think it is happening again now. The precipitation in the Southwest has been declining since the early 2000s. Stream flow and groundwater are reduced. Reservoirs are low. The drought that has settled over the Southwest could be part of the overall change in the worldwide climate. People in the Southwest should be prepared to use less water. And they should be aware that a general drying of the land could result in more and hotter wildfires.

The Role of the Ocean in West Coast Weather

The Pacific Ocean affects west coast weather in several ways. Most important, the ocean is the source of most of the water used in the west coast states. Water evaporates from the ocean, particularly where the Sun has warmed the ocean's surface. Wind carries the water vapor and clouds over the land. As the moist air rises and cools over the coastal mountains, the Sierra Nevada, and the Cascade Range, the vapor condenses and falls back to Earth's surface. During the spring and summer, the water flows back to the ocean, to complete the water cycle.

The ocean creates mild temperatures all year along the west coast. It rarely gets too hot or too cold. The temperature of the ocean doesn't change quickly. So the ocean acts to keep the air temperature near the coast even all year.

The ocean creates breezes near the coast. Because water heats up and cools down slowly, there is often a difference in the temperature of the land and the ocean. Uneven heating starts a convection current in motion, which results in wind. The ocean is responsible for sea breezes.

Review Questions

1. **What causes tornadoes?**

2. **What causes hurricanes?**

3. **How does the water cycle affect weather along the west coast?**

4. **How does the ocean influence the weather along the west coast?**

Weather Maps

Scientists who study weather are called meteorologists. They collect information about the condition of the atmosphere. Meteorologists measure air temperature, moisture content (humidity), and air pressure. They measure wind speed and precipitation. They keep track of the movements of masses of warm and cold air.

But there is more to the meteorologists' job. They want to know more than what the weather is today. They want to predict what the weather will be like tomorrow and the day after tomorrow. Predicting weather is called forecasting.

Meteorologists use information from surface measurements, atmospheric measurements, and satellite images. Information from all three sources is analyzed to make a forecast.

Surface Measurements

Weather data are collected every hour at over 300 stations across the United States. At these locations, meteorologists measure several **weather variables,** including temperature, wind speed and direction, air pressure, cloud cover, and precipitation. These data are fed into weather service computers. The computers generate surface-weather maps.

The surface-weather map has a code at each of the measuring stations. The code is a combination of numbers and symbols. Information about all the weather variables can be read for each station.

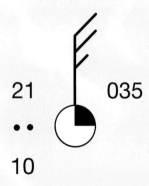

Here's how the information is coded.

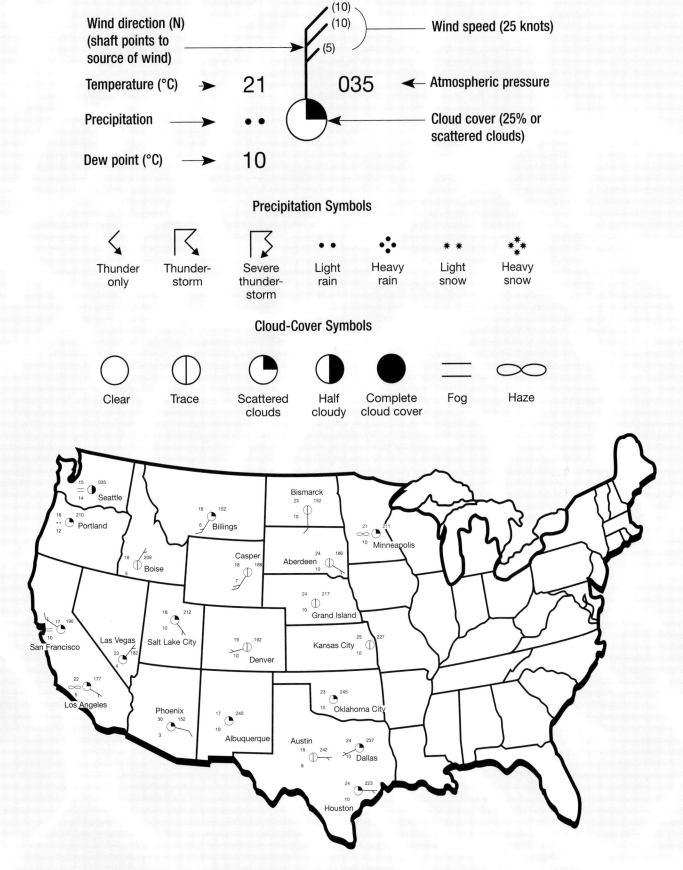

Wind direction (N) (shaft points to source of wind)

Wind speed (25 knots)

Temperature (°C) → 21   035 ← Atmospheric pressure

Precipitation → • •

Cloud cover (25% or scattered clouds)

Dew point (°C) → 10

Precipitation Symbols

Thunder only   Thunder-storm   Severe thunder-storm   Light rain   Heavy rain   Light snow   Heavy snow

Cloud-Cover Symbols

Clear   Trace   Scattered clouds   Half cloudy   Complete cloud cover   Fog   Haze

Meteorologists take readings from ground instruments.

Meteorologists release a weather balloon with a radiosonde.

Atmospheric Measurements

Weather balloons carry instruments into the upper atmosphere to make observations twice daily. The balloons are released at exactly the same time all over the world. There are 93 release stations in the United States. In Washington state, the balloons go up at 4:00 a.m. and 4:00 p.m. In Pennsylvania, the balloons go up at 7:00 a.m. and 7:00 p.m.

The balloons carry **radiosondes,** instruments that measure temperature, pressure, and humidity of the air. The radiosonde sends the information to the station until the balloon pops. Meteorologists also track the balloon's path to figure out wind speed and direction.

Satellite Images

Earth is surrounded by satellites parked in place about 35,000 kilometers (22,000 miles) above Earth's surface. These satellites "watch" the clouds and water vapor move over Earth's surface. They read the temperature of Earth's surface. They identify the storm centers. All this information is sent back to Earth. Meteorologists use powerful computers to change the signals from the satellites into images of Earth's weather.

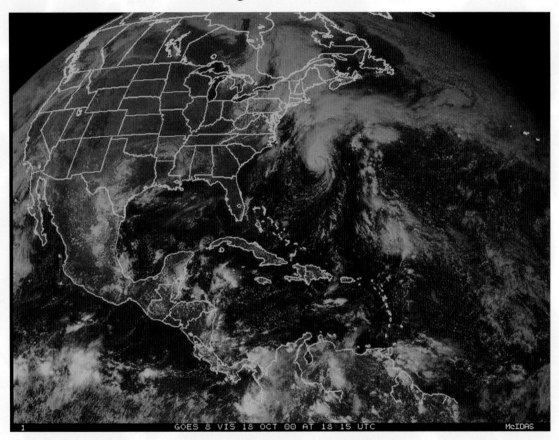

GOES 8 VIS 18 OCT 00 AT 18:15 UTC   McIDAS

Making Weather Maps

Meteorologists bring together the information from surface measurements, atmospheric measurements, and satellite images. Then they make **weather maps.** A weather map is a way to show weather data as a picture. A basic weather map is a picture of high and low pressure, temperatures, and places where masses of warm and cold air meet. With this information on a map, a meteorologist can make a good weather forecast.

Reading Weather Maps

The Sun heats Earth's surface more near the equator than at the poles. Huge masses of air over the Caribbean Sea become warm. At the same time, huge masses of air in Alaska and northern Canada become cold. The masses of cold air move south, and the masses of warm air move north. When they meet, the area of contact is called a **front.** Weather changes happen at fronts.

A **cold front** happens when a cold air mass overtakes a mass of warm, moist air. When this happens, the cold air pushes under the warm air and pushes it into the upper atmosphere very rapidly. The warm air cools, water condenses, and a thunderstorm occurs. If the temperature difference between the air masses is large, a tornado might develop.

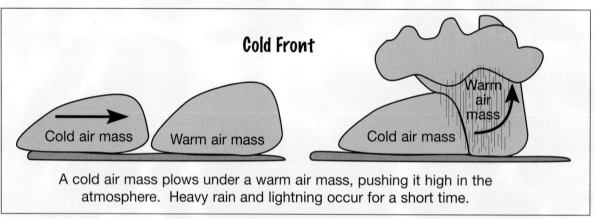

A cold air mass plows under a warm air mass, pushing it high in the atmosphere. Heavy rain and lightning occur for a short time.

A **warm front** happens when a warm air mass overtakes a cold air mass. The warm air slides over the top of the cold air in a long, slanting wedge. The warm air rises and cools slowly, and water vapor condenses into liquid over a long time. Warm fronts produce light rain for a long time.

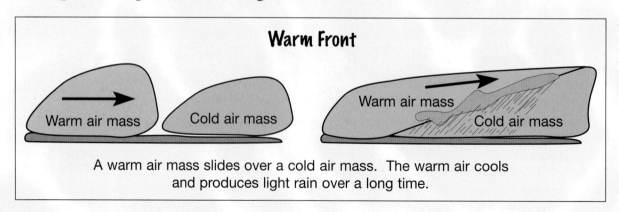

A warm air mass slides over a cold air mass. The warm air cools and produces light rain over a long time.

A line with points on a weather map shows where a cold front is. The points show which direction the cold front is moving. A line with round bumps is used to show where a warm front is. The side of the line with the bumps is the direction the warm front is moving. When the map is prepared in color, cold fronts are blue and warm fronts are red.

Sometimes a warm front and a cold front come together and stop moving. This is called a **stationary front.** It is shown by a line with points on one side and bumps on the other. The weather under a stationary front is similar to the weather produced by a cold front.

High-pressure areas are shown on a weather map with a large letter *H*. Low-pressure areas are shown by a large letter *L*.

H L

The weather around a high-pressure center is usually cool and dry. That's because high pressure is associated with denser air. Denser air tends to be cool and dry.

Low-pressure areas are usually warmer and moist. That's because low pressure is associated with less-dense air.

When a low-pressure area is near a high-pressure area, air will move from the high-pressure area to the low-pressure area. The movement of air is wind. The weather around a low-pressure area is windy and possibly rainy. As the warm air rises, cools, and condenses into clouds, it could start to rain.

Look at the three weather maps for Monday, September 19, 2005. Look at the large cold front going from Texas to New York. The upper part of the front moves across several states in the East. The southern end of the front, however, is stationary.

In map 1, a cold front meets a warm front in Canada. Warm, moist air rises and condenses. The forecast is for rain.

In map 2, a low-pressure area developed over the Dakotas Monday afternoon. Air from the high-pressure area over the Rocky Mountains in Colorado might flow across Wyoming and Nebraska to the low-pressure area. The forecast is for wind.

Look at map 3. What is the weather in California? There is a low-pressure area in southern California. Cool, moist air from the ocean is flowing toward the low-pressure area. If the moist air warms and rises as it approaches the warm low-pressure area, it could cool and condense. The forecast is for clouds and possible showers.

Look in the lower right-hand corner of the maps. There is a symbol that looks like this.

That is the symbol for a tropical storm or hurricane. This is Hurricane Rita. It is traveling past the southern tip of Florida not even a month after Hurricane Katrina hit the Gulf Coast. The forecast is for extreme wind and rain.

Monday
morning
8:00 a.m.

Map 1

Monday
afternoon
2:00 p.m.

Map 2

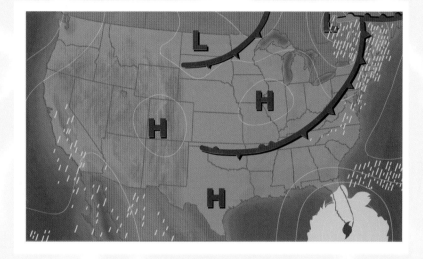

Monday
evening
8:00 p.m.

Map 3

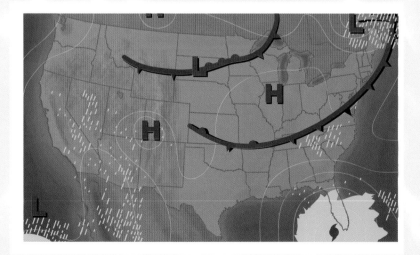

At National Weather Service forecast offices all around the United States, meteorologists use their skill and experience to produce weather forecasts. They consider all the weather variables such as air pressure, temperature, moisture, and wind. And they use their knowledge of general weather patterns.

Meteorologists know that winds in the upper atmosphere blow from west to east over most of the United States. So they know that most big weather systems also move from west to east.

They also know that air flows from high-pressure areas to low-pressure areas. This creates wind. So they look for high- and low-pressure areas on the weather map to figure out which way and how hard the wind will blow.

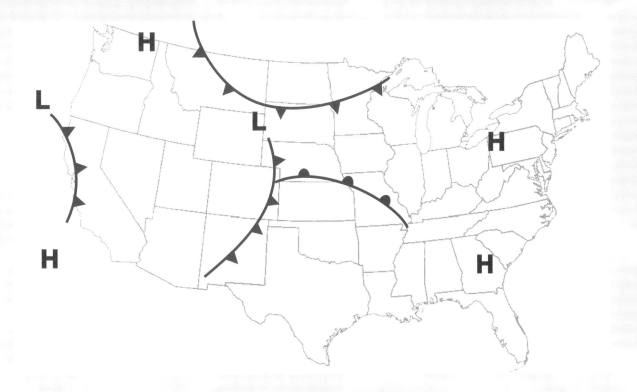

Review Questions

1. **What weather variables do meteorologists measure when they are preparing to make a weather forecast?**

2. **Describe three kinds of fronts and the weather they produce.**

3. **What causes wind?**

4. **Look at the sample weather map above. Where do you think it is raining? Where will it be raining tomorrow?**

5. **Look at the high- and low-pressure centers on the map above. Where do you think the wind is blowing? What direction?**

6. **Where is it likely to be cold and dry?**

Summary: Weather

Earth has weather. Three things cause the weather. First, Earth is just 150 million kilometers (93 million miles) away from a star, the Sun. Sunshine is the energy source that makes weather happen.

Second, Earth has an atmosphere made of air. This is where weather happens. Weather is what's happening in the atmosphere at any given time and place.

Third, Earth has water. Seventy-one percent of Earth's surface is covered by water. Most of Earth's weather has something to do with water.

Water Cycle

One thing weather does is move water around the planet. Most of Earth's water is **salt water.** Only 3% is **fresh water.** And only a small amount of the fresh water is available to plants and animals living on the land surfaces of Earth. People depend on that little bit of Earth's water for survival.

Will we run out of water? No, because it is recycled all the time by the **water cycle.** Water on Earth's surface evaporates and enters the atmosphere as water vapor, a gas. The most important source of evaporating water is the oceans. When water vapor rises in the atmosphere and cools, it condenses into liquid water. Clouds  made of countless droplets of water drift around the planet. When droplets form drops or ice crystals, they fall back to Earth's surface as **rain, snow, sleet,** or **hail.**

Severe Weather

Weather is defined by several **weather variables.** Weather variables describe the conditions of the atmosphere in a location on Earth. They include temperature, humidity, pressure, wind, and precipitation. Most of the time these variables fall within safe and comfortable limits. The weather might be rainy and windy, but not dangerous.

Sometimes one or more weather variables become extreme. This results in **severe weather.** Examples of severe weather include **tornadoes, hurricanes, thunderstorms, drought,** heat, and cold. Severe weather is dangerous to living organisms and can destroy property.

Hurricanes are powerful storms that form over warm water in late summer. The winds circling a hurricane's eye can reach speeds of 250 kilometers per hour (155 miles per hour). The energy that drives the storm is drawn from ocean water heated by the Sun. When a hurricane reaches land, the destruction caused by the wind and the flooding can be terrible.

A hurricane

A tornado

Thunderstorms and tornadoes form when a warm air mass and a cold air mass meet. The warm air is pushed upward rapidly. Lightning and heavy rain follow. When conditions are right, a spinning tornado can form. Winds in a tornado can reach speeds of more than 400 kilometers per hour (250 miles per hour). This makes tornadoes violent and dangerous storms on Earth.

Meteorologists study weather. One thing they try to do is to predict what the weather will be in the future. This is called forecasting. To make accurate forecasts, meteorologists have to collect a lot of weather data. Data are collected in three ways. Meteorologists measure weather variables at Earth's surface in hundreds of locations using weather instruments. They measure weather variables in the atmosphere in hundreds of locations, using weather balloons and **radiosondes.** And they study images sent to Earth by weather satellites. All of these data are sent to supercomputers.

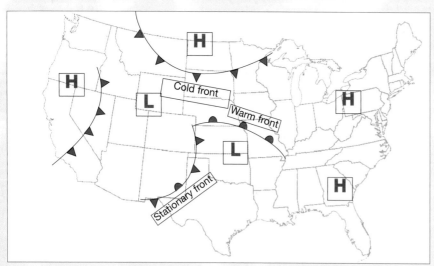

Meteorologists then make **weather maps** from the computer output. A weather map is a picture of the conditions of the atmosphere. It shows the high- and low-pressure areas. It shows where it is raining or snowing. It shows **warm fronts, cold fronts,** and **stationary fronts.** Experienced meteorologists can use weather maps to forecast the next day's weather.

Summary Questions

Now is a good time to review what you have recorded in your science notebook. Think about the weather investigations you conducted.

1. **Where is the water on Earth?**

2. **Describe how your region's water supply is refreshed by the water cycle.**

3. **What are some of the ways the ocean affects weather?**

Vocabulary

salt water

fresh water

water cycle

rain

snow

sleet

hail

weather variables

severe weather

tornado

hurricane

thunderstorm

drought

radiosonde

weather map

warm front

cold front

stationary front

References

Learning More about the Water Planet

The Planets

Visit a Planetarium

If there is a planetarium in your community, plan a visit. Check for presentations on the solar system, space exploration, or specific planets.

Plan a Visit with a Sidewalk Astronomer

You will find sidewalk astronomers in many communities who are willing to share their telescopes and knowledge. Visit the FOSSweb site for sidewalk astronomy resources.

Create a Travel Brochure

Choose a planet you would visit if you could. Design a travel brochure with descriptions of features, images, and tour information. Come up with a tour cost, too.

Find Out about Eratosthenes

Eratosthenes was a librarian who lived in Greece during the 3rd century B.C.E. He was the first person to calculate the circumference of Earth. Find out how Eratosthenes measured Earth and what effect his calculations might have had on Christopher Columbus's voyage to the Americas. *The Librarian Who Measured the Earth* by Kathryn Lasky is a good book to start with.

Create a Space-Exploration Timeline

Research the history of space exploration by the United States and other countries. Create a timeline that includes major events in space exploration.

Weather and Water

Research Recycling Water

The National Aeronautics and Space Administration (NASA) is working on ways to recycle water for astronauts in space. Research how NASA plans to do this.

- How many ways do astronauts use water?

- Why is it important for them to be able to recycle water?

Research Water Storage and Delivery Systems

Many areas of the United States store water in reservoirs. Find out where your water is stored and how it gets to your home and school. What effect does evaporation have on water storage?

Find the Condensation Temperature

Water vapor will not condense on a cup of warm water. Water vapor will condense on a cup of ice water. Somewhere between warm water and ice water is the temperature at which vapor will first condense. Find that temperature. The temperature is called dew point.

Investigate Solar Heating of Different Materials

Think of earth materials that have properties different from those you studied in class. Find out how the different properties affect temperature change. You might start with light and dark sand or water of different colors.

Research Temperatures around the World

Use the newspaper to keep track of temperatures for five cities for 2 weeks. Compare temperature data from coastal cities and inland cities. Which cities have the biggest temperature variations? Why? Pick a city and graph its temperature day by day all year.

Look for Severe Weather Now

Severe weather is occurring somewhere right now. Go to a news source or weather website to find out about severe windstorms (tornadoes, cyclones, monsoons, typhoons), heavy thunderstorms, and temperature extremes. Use a world map to display the current weather extremes.

FOSSweb

Go to www.FOSSweb.com to find activities for each FOSS module. You will also find interesting books to read, vocabulary lists, and links to related websites. This site was designed for you to use with friends and family at home. For your parents, there is information about each FOSS module and copies of the Home/School Connections.

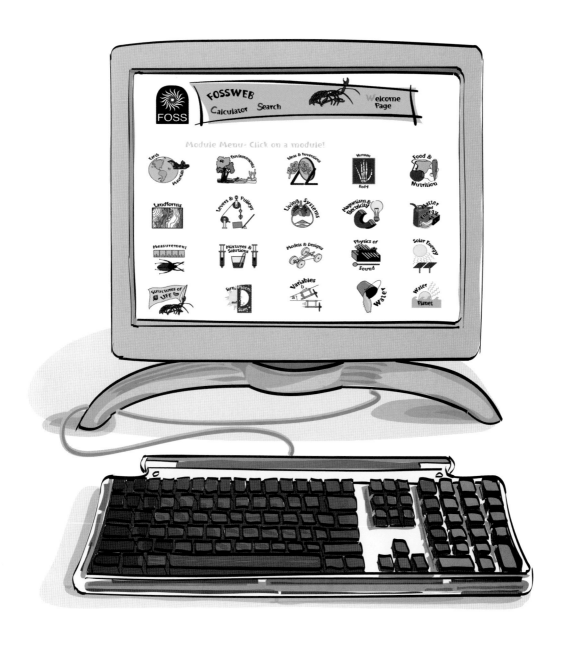

Science Safety Rules

1. Listen carefully to your teacher's instructions. Follow all directions. Ask questions if you don't know what to do.

2. Tell your teacher if you have any allergies.

3. Never put any materials in your mouth. Do not taste anything unless your teacher tells you to do so.

4. Never smell any unknown material. If your teacher tells you to smell something, wave your hand over the material to bring the smell toward your nose.

5. Do not touch your face, mouth, ears, eyes, or nose while working with chemicals, plants, or animals.

6. Always protect your eyes. Wear safety goggles when necessary. Tell your teacher if you wear contact lenses.

7. Always wash your hands with soap and warm water after handling chemicals, plants, or animals.

8. Never mix any chemicals unless your teacher tells you to do so.

9. Report all spills, accidents, and injuries to your teacher.

10. Treat animals with respect, caution, and consideration.

11. Clean up your work space after each investigation.

12. Act responsibly during all science activities.

Glossary

Air   The mixture of gases surrounding Earth.

Asteroid   Small, solid objects that orbit the Sun. Most of the asteroids in the solar system are located between Mars and Jupiter.

Astronomy   The study of the universe and its celestial bodies.

Atmosphere   The layer of gases that surrounds a planet or star.

Atmospheric pressure   The force exerted on a surface by the mass of the air above it.

Atom   The smallest particle of an element that has the properties of the element and can exist either alone or in combination with a similar atom as a molecule.

Blizzard   A severe storm with low temperatures, strong winds, and large quantities of snow.

Chemical property   A characteristic of an element that relates to how it interacts with other elements.

Cloud   Tiny droplets of water, usually high in the air.

Cold front   The contact zone where a cold air mass overtakes a mass of warm, moist air.

Comet   A mass of ice and dust orbiting the Sun.

Condensation   The process by which water vapor changes into liquid water, usually on a surface.

Conserve   To use carefully and protect.

Convection current   A circular movement of fluid (such as air) that is the result of uneven heating of the fluid.

Crater   A hole formed by an object impacting a surface.

Dew   Water that condenses on surfaces when the temperature drops at night.

Diameter   The straight-line distance from one side to the other side of an object through the center.

Drought   Less-than-normal amount of rain or snow over a period of time.

Dwarf planet   A round object that orbits the Sun but does not orbit a planet (so it is not a moon). It is not big enough to sweep up the other objects along its orbit.

Earth   The third planet from the Sun, known as the water planet.

Elevation   The distance above sea level.

Energy transfer   The movement of energy from one place to another, or the change of energy from one form to another.

Evaporate   To change from liquid to gas.

Evaporation   The process by which a liquid becomes a gas.

Extraterrestrial   Beyond Earth.

Fog   Water droplets that condense from the air close to the ground.

Forecasting   Predicting future events or conditions, such as weather.

Freezing point   The temperature at which a liquid turns into a solid (also the same temperature as the melting point).

Fresh water   Water without salt that is found in lakes, rivers, groundwater, soil, and the atmosphere.

Front   The leading edge of a moving air mass.

Frost   Frozen condensation.

Gas   A state of a substance with no definite shape or volume.

Gas giant   Any of the four planets that are made of gas. These are Jupiter, Saturn, Uranus, and Neptune.

Glacier   A huge mass of ice that moves slowly over land.

Gravitational attraction   The mutual force of attraction between all bodies that have mass.

Gravity   The force of attraction between two objects.

Hail   Precipitation in the form of small balls or pellets of ice.

Helium   A gas that makes up 26% of the Sun.

Humidity   Water vapor in the air.

Hurricane   A severe tropical storm or moving wind system that rotates around an eye, or center of low atmospheric pressure.

Hydrogen   A gas that makes up 72% of the Sun.

Intensity   How concentrated energy is.

Jupiter   The fifth planet from the Sun.

Kuiper Belt   A huge region beyond the gas giants made up of different-size icy chunks of matter.

Liquid   A state of a substance with no definite shape but definite volume.

Mars   The fourth planet from the Sun.

Mass   The amount of material in something.

Mercury   The planet closest to the Sun.

Meteorologist   A scientist who studies the weather.

Milky Way   The galaxy in which the solar system resides.

Moon   Earth's natural satellite.

Neptune   The eighth planet from the Sun.

Orbit   To travel in a curved path around something else.

Planet   A large body orbiting a star. A celestial body.

Pluto   A dwarf planet in the Kuiper Belt.

Precipitation   Rain, snow, sleet, or hail that falls to the ground.

Predictable   Possible to estimate a future event based on data or experience.

Radiosonde   An instrument sent into Earth's atmosphere to measure temperature, pressure, and humidity.

Rain   Liquid water that is condensed from water vapor in the atmosphere and falls to Earth in drops.

Recycle To use again.

Reflected Energy that bounces off an object and continues in a new direction.

Salt water Ocean water.

Satellite An object, natural or artificial, that orbits a larger object. Moons are satellites.

Saturated When the air cannot hold any more water vapor.

Saturn The sixth planet from the Sun.

Severe weather Out-of-the-ordinary and extreme weather conditions.

Sleet Precipitation in the form of ice pellets created when rain freezes as it falls to Earth from the atmosphere.

Snow Precipitation in the form of ice crystals grouped together as snowflakes.

Solar energy Heat and light from the Sun.

Solar system The planet Earth, the Moon, the Sun, and seven other planets and their satellites, and smaller objects, such as asteroids and comets.

Solar wind The regular flow of particles from the Sun.

Star A huge gas sphere that radiates light. The Sun is a star.

Stationary front When a warm air mass and a cold air mass come together and stop moving.

Sun The star at the center of the solar system around which everything else orbits. Also called Sol.

Surface area The amount of space covering the topmost layer of water or land.

Surface water Fresh water on Earth's surface, such as that in lakes and rivers.

Terrestrial planet One of the four small and rocky planets closest to the Sun. These are Mercury, Venus, Earth, and Mars.

Thermonuclear reactions Reactions that change atomic structure and create heat and light energy, such as the reactions that occur on the Sun.

Thunderstorm   Severe weather that results from cold air flowing under a warm, humid air mass over the land.

Tornado   A rapidly rotating column of air that extends from a thunderstorm to the ground. Wind speeds can reach more than 400 kilometers per hour (250 mph) in a tornado.

Uneven heating   The result of different amounts of energy being transferred to adjacent surfaces.

Uranus   The seventh planet from the Sun.

Venus   The second planet from the Sun.

Warm front   The contact zone where a warm air mass overtakes a cold air mass.

Water cycle   The global water-recycling system. Water evaporates from Earth's surface, goes into the atmosphere, and condenses. It returns to Earth's surface as precipitation in a new location.

Water molecule   Two hydrogen atoms and one oxygen atom bonded together.

Water vapor   Water in its gas form.

Weather   The condition of the atmosphere around us. Heat, moisture, and movement are the three important variables that describe weather.

Weather forecast   A prediction of future weather conditions.

Weather map   A map that shows weather data as a picture.

Weather variable   Data that meteorologists measure. These include temperature, wind speed and direction, air pressure, cloud cover, and precipitation.

Wind   Air in motion.

Index

Gravity
   and almost-circular orbits around Sun,
      21
   defined, 16, 103
   described, 16–17
   space shuttle in orbit, 19
Great Red Spot, 9
Groundwater
   amount of water in Earth's, 63
   defined, 64
   and drought, 77–78
   use of, 65
   See also Underground water
Gulf Coast, 71, 73, 86
Gulf of Mexico, 71, 75

H

Hail, 69, 90, 103
Hawaiian Islands, 7, 77
Heating
   atmospheric pressure, 59–61
   convection currents and wind, 59
   of Earth's surface, 43, 58–59
   uneven, 49, 51, 57–59, 79, 105
   as weather variable, 72
   See also Solar energy; Uneven heating;
      Variable
Helium
   composition of Saturn, 10
   defined, 103
   in Jupiter's atmosphere, 9
   in Neptune, 11
   and Sun, 3, 20
Home/School Connection, 25, 41, 62
Hot-air molecules, 47
Household, use of water, 65–66
Humidity, 41, 72, 80, 103
Hurricane
   defined, 73, 102
   as example of severe weather, 72, 91
   Katrina, 71, 73, 86
   Linda, 73
   Rita, 86

symbol for, 86
and uneven heating, 51
Hydrogen (H)
   composition of Saturn, 10
   defined, 103
   in Jupiter's atmosphere, 9
   in Neptune's atmosphere, 11
   and Sun, 3, 20, 23

I

Ida, 8
Identify, 62
Industry, use of water, 65–66
Intensity, 43, 103
Io, 9
Iron oxide, 7

J

Jemison, Mae, 18–19
Jupiter
   craters created from Comet
      Shoemaker-Levy 9, 13
   defined, 103
   described, 9
   gas giant, 8, 21
   orbit in Earth days, 24
   relative size, 22
   visible at night, 25

K

Kilogram, 52, 53
Kilometer, 6, 10, 16, 19
Kuiper Belt, 1
   defined, 21, 103
   Eris, 12
   Pluto, 12, 21

L

Lakes
   amount of water in Earth's, 63
   and drought, 77
   and evaporation, 33
   fresh water in, 64, 93
Libya, 76

S

Salt water, 64, 90, 104. *See also* Ocean(s)

San Clemente, California, 44, 46

Sand, 44

San Francisco, California, 39, 71

Satellites
 defined, 104
 images, 80, 83
 of Jupiter, 9
 of Mars, 7
 of Mercury, 4
 orbits around sun, 20
 of Pluto, 12
 of Saturn, 10
 of Venus, 5
 See also Moon

Saturated
 defined, 30, 39, 104
 described, 36

Saturn
 defined, 104
 described, 10
 as gas giant, 8, 21
 orbit in Earth days, 24
 relative size, 22
 rings, 21
 Uranus compared to, 11
 visible at night, 25

Sea level, 60

Severe weather, 91–92
 causes of, 72
 defined, 104, 91
 examples of, 71–72, 91
 hot and cold, 76
 hurricanes and tropical storms, 51, 71, 73, 86, 91, 103
 thunderstorms, 51, 72, 74, 84, 91, 96
 tornadoes, 51, 72, 75, 84, 91, 96, 105
 western weather extremes, 76–79

Sierra Nevada, 54, 79

Sleet, 69, 90, 104

Snow
 defined, 104
 in Ohio River Valley, 68–69
 in space, 15

water cycle, 90
water vapor, 90
weather in Midwest and East, 71
western weather extremes, 76–77

Soil moisture, 63, 64, 77

Sojourner, 7

Sol, 3, 20. *See also* Sun

Solar energy
 cooling land without, 50
 defined, 42–45, 104
 for Earth, 6
 heating land, 47
 See also Sun

Solar flares, 15

Solar system
 asteroids, 1, 8
 comets, 13
 defined, 1, 20, 104
 Earth, 6, 22
 Eris, 12
 gas giants, 1, 8–11
 Jupiter, 9, 22
 Kuiper Belt, 1, 12
 Mars, 7, 22
 Mercury, 4, 22
 Moon, 26
 Neptune, 11, 22
 objects visible with bare eyes at night, 25
 Pluto, 12, 22
 relative sizes of planets in, 22
 Saturn, 10, 22
 star, 1
 Sun, 2–3
 terrestrial planets, 1, 4–7
 Uranus, 11, 22
 Venus, 5, 22

Solar wind, 15, 104

Solid(s), as state of matter, 38

Space weather, 15

Spirit, 7

Stanford University, 18

Star, 1–3, 20, 42, 104. *See also* Sun

Static electricity, 74

Stationary front, 85–86, 92, 104

112

STS-47, 18–19

Sun
    age, 3
    and asteroid belt, 21
    composed of hydrogen and helium, 3,
       20
    defined, 104
    described, 2–3
    as driver of water cycle, 68
    as driver of weather, 90–91
    as Earth's closest star, 20
    Earth's orbit around, 16
    Earth's proximity to, 6
    and energy to change water into
       vapor, 70
    energy to create heat from, 76
    energy to create wind from, 46
    equator and poles, 84
    Eris's proximity to, 12
    everything in solar system orbits, 2
    formation of, 3
    and gravity, 16–17, 21
    heat and light from, 42–45
    Jupiter's proximity to, 9
    Mars's proximity to, 7
    as mass, 3, 17
    Mercury's proximity to, 4
    Neptune's proximity to, 11
    orbit of comets, 13
    Pluto's proximity to, 12
    Saturn's proximity to, 10
    size of, 3
    and space weather, 15
    temperature of, 3
    and thunderstorms, 74
    Uranus' proximity to, 11
    Venus' proximity to, 5
    See also Solar energy; Star
Sunshine, weather and, 72
Surface area, 31–32, 38, 104
Surface measurements, 80–81
Surface water, 64–65, 104. See also Lakes;
    Rivers
Surface-weather map, 80–81

T

Temperature
    atmospheric, 57
    of Earth's surface, 43–45, 83
    measuring, 80–81
    ocean and coastal, 79
    thunderstorms and tornadoes, 84
    tracking, 96
    as weather variable, 80
    See also Cooling; Heating
Terrestrial planets
    asteroids, 8
    defined, 1, 104
    Earth, 6, 20
    Mars, 7, 20
    Mercury, 4, 20
    relative sizes, 22
    separated from gas giants by asteroid
       belt, 21
    Venus, 5, 20
Texas, 75, 78, 86
Thermonuclear reaction, 3, 104
Thunderstorm, 51, 72, 84, 91, 105
Tornado, 51, 72, 75–76, 84, 91, 105
Tornado Alley, 75
Transfer, energy, 47, 58, 102
Tropical storm, 73, 86
Tropics, 45

U

Underground water, 64
Uneven heating, 42–45
    and air touching Earth's surface, 72
    defined, 105
    and solar energy, 45, 58
    and weather changes, 51, 72
    and wind, 59, 79
    See also Convection current
United States, 75, 82, 88
Uranus
    defined, 105
    described, 11
    gas giant, 8, 21

Photo Credits

Cover & Page i: NASA; **Page 1:** Rose Craig/Lawrence Hall of Science; **Page 2:** NASA/JPL; **Page 4:** Lawrence Hall of Science (top); NASA/JPL/Northwestern University (bottom); **Pages 5–7:** NASA/JPL (all); **Page 8:** NASA/JPL/USGS (top); NASA/JPL; **Page 9:** NASA/JPL (background, top right, center left, middle and right); NASA/JPL/University of Arizona (bottom left); **Page 10:** NASA/JPL (both); **Page 11:** NASA/Hubble Space Telescope (left); NASA/JPL (right); **Page 12:** NASA/JPL (top); NASA/JPL-Caltech (bottom); **Page 13:** Dennis diCicco/CORBIS (top); NASA/Hubble Space Telescope (center); NASA (bottom); **Page 15:** NASA/JPL (left); Courtesy, Ellen Lopez (right); **Pages 16–17:** Rose Craig/Lawrence Hall of Science; **Pages 18–19:** Johnson Space Center/NASA (all); **Page 20:** NASA/JPL; **Page 21:** Rose Craig/Lawrence Hall of Science; **Page 22:** NASA/JPL; **Page 26:** Lawrence Hall of Science (both, top); © David Young Wolff/Photo Edit (bottom); **Pages 28–29:** Rose Craig/Lawrence Hall of Science (all); **Page 33:** Lawrence Hall of Science; **Page 34:** Rose Craig/Lawrence Hall of Science; **Page 35:** © Stephen Ingram/Animals Animals (top); © Gary Griffen/Animals Animals/Earth Scenes (bottom left); © Tom Walker/Visuals Unlimited (bottom right); **Page 36:** PhotoDisc, Inc. (top); Lawrence Hall of Science (center right); Punchstock (bottom); **Page 37:** © P. Parviainen/Photo Researchers, Inc. (left); © F. Stuart Westmorland/Photo Researchers, Inc. (right); **Page 38:** Rose Craig/Lawrence Hall of Science; **Page 39:** Lawrence Hall of Science; **Page 41:** Rose Craig/Lawrence Hall of Science; **Page 42:** Marco Molinaro/Lawrence Hall of Science; **Page 44:** © Tom Prettyman/Photo Edit; **Page 45:** Rose Craig/Lawrence Hall of Science; **Page 46:** © Myrleen Ferguson Cate/Photo Edit (top); Rose Craig/Lawrence Hall of Science (bottom); **Pages 47–65:** Rose Craig/Lawrence Hall of Science (all); **Page 67:** © Science VU/Visuals Unlimited (top right); © David Davis/Shutterstock; **Pages 68–69:** Rose Craig/Lawrence Hall of Science (all); **Page 71:** NOAA; **Page 73:** Weatherstock; **Page 74:** Courtesy of Air Force Military Archives (both); **Page 75:** NOAA Photo Library, NOAA Central Library; OAR/ERL/National Severe Storms Laboratory (NSSL); **Page 77:** GOES image/NOAA; **Page 78:** Susan Lindstrom; **Page 81:** Rose Craig/Lawrence Hall of Science; **Page 82:** © Stephen J. Krasemann/Photo Researchers, Inc. (left); © Mark C. Burnett/Photo Researchers, Inc. (right); **Page 83:** National Weather Service; **Pages 84–90:** Rose Craig/Lawrence Hall of Science (all); **Page 91:** NOAA (top right); NOAA Photo Library, NOAA Central Library; OAR/ERL/National Severe Storms Laboratory (NSSL) (bottom left); **Pages 92, 97, 99:** Rose Craig/Lawrence Hall of Science (all); **Page 95:** NASA. Delta Education has made every effort to trace the ownership of copyrighted images.

About the Cover: Earth